Pemba Tamang
written by Stuart Kirby

Finding the Way

A Journey Through Life and Karate

A PT publication

First published in 2014

Copyright © Pemba Tamang 2014

The rights of Pemba Tamang to be identified as the author of this work has been asserted by him in accordance with the Copyright, Designs and Patent Act 1988.

All rights reserved. No part of this publication may be reproduced, stored in a retrieval system, or transmitted, in any form or by any means, electronic, mechanical, photocopying, recording or otherwise, without the prior permission of the copyright owner.

Every effort has been made to fulfil requirements with regard to reproducing copyright material. The author and publisher will be glad to rectify any omissions at the earliest opportunity.

Front cover – painting of Kangchenjunga by Pemba Tamang

Contents

Part 1 – Life

Chapter 1 – Redemption

Chapter 2 – The Contract

Chapter 3 – Reality

Chapter 4 – Guilt

Chapter 5 – The First Peak

Chapter 6 – Kenshusei

Chapter 7 – The Break Up

Chapter 8 – Flying High

Chapter 9 – Fallen

Chapter 10 – Getting Up

Chapter 11 – Deep in Nature

Part 2 - Understanding

Chapter 12 – My Way

Chapter 13 – Recognition

Chapter 14 – Zen Ku Mon

Part 3 - Application

Chapter 15 – Pre Training Techniques

Chapter 16 – Gyaku zuki

Chapter 17 – Oi zuki

Chapter 18 – Mae Geri

Chapter 19 – Mawashi Geri

Chapter 20 – Continuation Techniques

Preface

Gichin Funakoshi, the founder of modern karate, wrote a number of guiding principles that he encouraged his students to live by. One of those principles was, '*Jinkaku kansei ni tsutomoru koto*' which in English translates to mean 'Seek perfection in character,' or as I interpreted it, 'polish your character until you find completeness.' As I passed my fiftieth birthday I realised that living by this principle is not as easy as it might sound!

I have been very fortunate to have found karate very early on in my life and the training and guiding principles have helped me steer my life, for the most part, in a positive direction, though like many of your reading this, there have also been some dark times.

'Finding the Way' is my story of how I came to discover much about karate, Japan and ultimately myself. I hope my experiences will provide some guidance to others and not just on the subject of karate.

The first part of this book focuses on my life as I go from a boy growing up in Nepal and India to an international karate instructor. There are many highs and lows, struggles and challenges, none of which I regret, as they have made me who I am. Part two attempts to decipher these experiences into a philosophy that I hope makes sense to the reader and helps them find their 'Way' through life. Finally part three is for the karate student as I share the principles I've learnt from practicing karate for more than forty years and learning from some of the greatest karate masters of Japan.

Finally, I would like to say a big thank you and express my appreciation and respect to all those that have been such an influence in my life, including my sensei's (teachers,) senpai (senior,) friends and of course my family for their loving support over the years, especially my wife Mari for all her help with the editing of this book, and a special thanks to Stuart Kirby whose strong friendship, understanding and writing skills made this book possible. I hope my story can serve as help to others as they find their 'way' through life.

Pemba Tamang

Chapter 1 Redemption

The wind was picking up, echoing that eerie sound that nature likes to play across a wind swept mountain. The cold bit down hard on our hands and faces, and the sinking sun gave us barely enough light and time to finish our task.

'Dig faster Madan, dig faster,' I urged. I wasn't hurrying because I was cold or scared of the dark. This was the hundredth body we had buried over the past few months, and yet I had such a bad feeling about it that I felt compelled to keep glancing back over my shoulder as though the grim reaper himself would suddenly appear.

There were only three of us available that afternoon: Binod, Madan and myself, which made the two hour trek to the mountainside graveyard even harder. The only benefit of being a trio was that we didn't carry the body on our shoulders, the usual formation for four grave diggers. Instead, we carried the body stretcher-style and rotated the third man. This way any bodily fluids that left the deceased would fall to the ground, instead of down our necks (as had happened on many occasions) sending greater shivers down our spines.

We had gone to the hospital around 3 p.m. and been directed by the nurses to 'the room.' 'The room' conjured up such terrifying images for us that we couldn't bring ourselves to think about it long enough to give it a name, so it remained 'the room.' Entering 'the room' required more courage than any one of us had, so we had made a pact to turn the key, count to three and then charge in together. On this occasion, as we thrust the door open, our eyes immediately met with the deceased; the nurses had forgotten to cover the head, and his eyes stared coldly into the abyss. The pact was broken; no one charged in.

'I'm not going in there, I don't care what you say but I'm not going in there! This is the one time I say no. You know me Pemba, I never say no, but today I say no.'

It was true, Binod was brave and as solid as the mountains that looked over our town, but even he could not face this man with advanced decomposition, facial muscles wasted, revealing droopy skin, soon to expose the bone.

'MADAN, WE GO,' I shouted, hoping that by raising my voice it would summon some kind of extra courage in me. Madan was known to talk bravely, but his talk didn't always match his actions, but this time he didn't let me down.

'You take the feet, I'll get the shoulders,' I instructed. It was either clumsy tiredness or rushing through fear, but I mistakenly placed both hands above the shoulder blades, not under the shoulder blades as I should have, and consequently my fingers slid clean through, into the rotting flesh.

'Erhh, oh shit! Madan what should I do?'

'Wash your hands, Pemba' was the response from the ever-practical Madan. But this experience had seriously unnerved me, I'd entered the flesh of another and it would not matter how hard I scrubbed my fingers I would not wash away the feeling, the memory.

All three of us left the hospital carrying the body and walked solemnly for two hours to the mountain graveyard. The silence tortured me, allowing my mind to play the event over and over.

Maybe I should have made conversation to calm us all but I was in such a state of shock; conversation would seem futile. The silence did allow me time to once again contemplate why I had volunteered for this job, a job that was so macabre that many people couldn't even bring themselves to talk about it, let alone make it a regular part of their lives. However, with regularity came acceptance so the job was not always full of such darkness, there were of course times of camaraderie and laughter, we were best friends working together under the strangest of circumstances. It was the laughter that kept us sane.

I remember one such occasion when I was new to the job, I'd arrived at the hospital with Binod and the body we had to collect had thankfully not made it to the 'room' yet. The nurse gave us the bed number and we made our way, joined by at least another seven volunteers to the bed where the deceased lay. Binod was carrying the customary cloth that we would wrap the body in and we unravelled it beside the dead man. I gave a whispered one, two, three, that time Binod had the shoulders and I the legs. We lifted the man when suddenly the corpse came to life and jolted, the panic and screams from that room must have alerted the whole hospital, but we were not around to see anyone, as Binod and I ran and ran and ran, followed by the other seven volunteers. We eventually stopped to catch our breath near the convent, a good half-mile from the hospital. We laughed and laughed as we tried desperately to catch our breath. The half a mile sprint had brought fresh oxygen to our brains, allowing us to logically conclude that we had in fact been given the wrong bed number and so it wasn't the start of a zombie outbreak, set to befall our town. The pensive atmosphere that always existed when we first approached a dead body left us vulnerable to our imaginations and I can only conclude that when the body moved, Binod, I, and the entire posse of volunteers could only focus our wayward logic on the zombie film that had recently been shown at the local picture house. Of course, it didn't help that the man that was sick and resting in the hospital bed was so ill he looked dead.

Our volunteer job as town undertakers and grave diggers paid us in hot tea and sweets and yet, it would burden us with a lifetime of disturbing memories. And so it was, we paid a huge price for our tea and sweets. Just the other night as we practiced the unfortunate but necessary rotation policy at the mountain burial site, digging up those plots that were at least five years old and replacing them with new corpses, we came across a corpse that couldn't have been more than a few months old and at a stomach-wrenching stage of decomposition. It was horrible.

Simply the most horrible experience of my short life, up until the moment of accidentally piercing a dead person's flesh with my own bare hands.

It may seem strange or even disrespectful to the dead, but rotating the burial places was a decision based on practical, not emotional terms. Digging deep holes throughout the mountain-side would have been extremely difficult considering the limited digging equipment we had, so it came to be that once the body had fully decayed to a skeleton, the hole could be used again. We had our customs of course: before laying the body in the hole we would place a coin there to signify to the spirit world that we were purchasing this land so the deceased could rest in peace. Strangely enough, my four years as voluntary grave digger, I never once recovered one of those coins used to purchase real estate in the after world.

'Dig faster Madan, dig faster,' I insisted again. The rocky soil seemed particularly hard that night, and the mist that covered the lower part of the mountain threw a spell over the area reminiscent of one of those Dracula-type horror films that had become popular in recent months. As always, the scent of Darjeeling tea was carried through the air mixed with the musty smell common among rotting corpses would have put even the most ardent of tea drinkers off the famous tea.

It was getting late, cold and my wits were wearing thinner and thinner. The snap of a twig, the creak of a tree, and the blood curdling howl from a nearby animal were further adding to my anxiety, but still Madan continued to dig at a steady pace.

Our friendship had grown stronger over the years. Although five years my senior, Binod was a delicate looking young man, but he was brave and surprisingly strong for his small frame, and thought carefully before he spoke, making what he said seem reasonable and wise, giving the impression that he was well above his years. Madan on the other hand was more like me: our mouths going into action before our brains. Madan liked to talk big, and even though it was Binod and I that attended to the majority of the dead, it was Madan who recounted the stories loudly in front of others. He seemed to enjoy telling these stories when in earshot of someone eating or a pretty girl he wanted to impress.

Facing death on a daily basis had begun with my own father's death just as I had turned thirteen. Losing my father so young had forced me to take stock of my barely begun life, and even though I was not the eldest of my three brothers and one sister, I felt inclined to provide for my family like my father once did. This of course meant my school work suffered more than usual, and even though I was working from the age of thirteen, I still managed to graduate school by studying for the exams on my own. I felt proud that I was helping my family, but still I had to do more in my father's memory, and this became part of my reasoning to volunteer my services to my town. So it was that I came to care for these beings that were beyond sick and elderly and even suicidal.

Growing up in a poor family in a small town called Darjeeling meant facing a lot of hardships but at the time we knew no different. I had an energy that was overly boisterous, bordering destructive, actually. I had given my parents many problems with my behaviour and my behaviour had given me many problems in return. My attempts at feigning illness to get out of school had reached such a height of creativity that consequently I was missing two rear teeth. I'd exhausted stomach pains, earache, sore throats, until there was nothing left on my body to complain about and every time my parents insisted I go to the doctor. Either they believed me too easily and felt I was a sickly child, or they looked to call my bluff by putting me in front of the doctor, but still I went, wasting the doctors' valuable time and receiving a huge range of medicine that I would wastefully discard. It seemed only natural to add 'toothache' to my long list of ailments, and was caught off-guard when the doctor thought the best course of action was to 'pull teeth'. It seemed a price worth paying though, as missing school allowed me more time and freedom to explore the mountain and of course get into more mischief. It was this mischief which had turned many of my friend's parents against me. They would even receive punishment if they were seen in my company. Eventually the whole town began to see me as a nuisance, a wild, unyielding tearaway.

      Volunteering would help me win respect from the town and allow my father to watch over me in peace. But this was not the only reason. The volunteer service was the only place in the town that had a clear, open space with a wooden floor. This was often used as a place for the town elders to meet and discuss important matters, and was offered to the volunteers to use freely when their chores were complete. It was here I was allowed to practice my passion, to practice something that absorbed my energy and kept it under some semblance of control. It was here I practiced karate.

(Pemba Tamang, his younger brothers and friends)

(Pemba Tamang, his mother and three younger brothers,)

Chapter 2 The Contract

I began karate at the age of ten, not because I was bullied, nor did I bully, but such was my character that I'd challenge anyone and anything. Naturally this would lead to fighting, often with older boys. I thought karate would help me prepare for these inevitable tussles, though interestingly, after just a couple of years of training I had completely lost the urge to challenge anyone outside of the dojo.

My sensei at the time was a good man and had a passion for what he was teaching, though it was far from what I'd one day learn about karate in Japan. My boisterous energy seemed to contain itself in these sessions and my attitude began to improve in all other areas of my life. I began to build a reputation in the dojo as being a strong fighter and with a great discipline for practice. I trained every day and made the most of the volunteer's hall for extra practice.

As I increased my karate training and volunteer work the attitude of the townsfolk began to change towards me, I began to win their respect and they finally trusted me enough to allow their loved ones to hang out with me. Gone were the days of stealing chickens and hiding out in the mountains with my gang as we pretended to be cowboys living off of the land. My karate reputation had further 'built me' into a trusted young man, some would even tell their restless children to go and practise karate with Pemba. It seemed that the small changes I'd made, starting karate training and volunteering, were beginning to have a huge impact on my life. Despite that, something continued to bother me.

Something about my karate training didn't seem right. We practiced a lot, but what we practised seemed to only have meaning in the sense of how it looked and not how it felt, almost like a dance. My karate didn't feel powerful; it felt like we were just imitating karate from a film. My inquisitive character wanted to search deeper into this art that I'd now been practicing for many years. I'd become thirsty to know more and unfortunately my sensei could not provide me with the substance I needed. My restless mind led me to talk big.

'I'll go to Japan and find the real karate and there I'll get my black belt,' I announced again to Binod and Madan as we returned from the mountain graveyard.

'Yes Pemba,' they said in chorus, knowing that I'd been repeating this chant for many months now. I'd told everybody: my mother, my brothers, my sister, neighbours everyone, even a Japanese tourist that we had raced after as he passed through town. I demanded, 'tell me about karate in Japan,' and was left in a state of shock and bewilderment on hearing that he had never practised karate or any of the Japanese martial arts for that matter.

Making such bold announcements came with a price: for four years everyone remembered my boasts about going to Japan and everyone reminded me, on what felt like a daily basis, I had yet to go. Some joked, 'How was Japan Pemba? It must have been a short trip, hey?'

I'd inadvertently made a contract with myself, if I failed to honour the contract I would be subject to a penalty. The penalty: gentle mocking from the townsfolk, forever. They'd already mocked me in the first instance, saying how crazy I was to think that a poor, small-town boy from Darjeeling could make it to Japan. Later in life, I realised that the contracts we make with ourselves come with a much higher penalty if left unhonoured. In fact, they can eat away at someone, reducing them to a life of misadventure and regret. On this occasion I honoured the contract, and after spending several years saving money, it was time to save face and go to Japan.

It was my first time on an airplane but it had an air of familiarity about it; I guess that's the power of films. We didn't have a TV in my town, but would often go to the picture house to see the latest Hindi film and sometimes even a Hollywood movie, though in those days few films were subtitled, so for us it was a visual experience. These visual experiences gave me a view away from our small town that was tucked away and hidden by the gaze of the Himalayas. However, all the films in the world couldn't prepare me for the actual experience of take-off or the forthcoming turbulence when crossing the Bay of Bengal as we made our way to Bangkok, my eyes darting from person to person, attempting to read if anyone else was in a state of panic. My first experience also left me blissfully unaware that the smiles and polite gestures coming from an air hostess was part of her job, for I'd sat in my seat for almost two hours wondering how to respond to her smiling advances. Me, a simple small-town boy from Darjeeling, and her, a beautiful woman of the world. I slipped into a light sleep, dreaming of the adventures that awaited me.

At Bangkok we changed planes and continued on to Taipei and then on to Hong Kong where I would spend my first night sleeping far away from my family, and in a foreign country at that. In my hometown there were some grand buildings left over from colonial rule of the British, but rarely did these buildings stretch higher than five stories, so when I first made my way through the streets of Hong Kong I was overwhelmed by the sheer size of the buildings looming up from where I stood. The lights, the cars, the hordes of people moving from street to street; crossing the road in orderly unison, a far cry from home where people and animals crossed where they liked. It made me feel even smaller and insignificant to the world I was about to discover more of. In those days it was not possible to take a direct flight from India to Japan, so I had to buy my final flight in Hong Kong. Fortunately for me the travel agent spoke English very well; laced with a British accent, he was the first to mention the need for something called a visa to enter Japan.

'A visa! What is this visa? I need one flight to Tokyo so I can train in karate and get my black belt,' I said impatiently.

'I understand Mr Tamang, but in order to enter Japan at the very least you require a tourist visa and unfortunately I cannot sell you a ticket until you have one,' he insisted with his Chinese face and British accent.

My mind was obsessed with achieving a black belt in karate. It seemed simple: I go to
Tokyo, find a dojo, train for two months, receive my black belt and return to the celebrations and admiration of my town. I'd neglected to plan for

the other details, such as a visa, hotel bookings, or even where I would stay in Tokyo, a city I anticipated to be only slightly bigger than my hometown.

The travel agent's advice was very useful, and after returning from the Japanese embassy over in Kowloon with visa in hand, he was happy to sell me a ticket to Tokyo arriving in Narita Airport in the early morning. After four flights I finally arrived at Narita ready to begin my karate training and gain my black belt.

Narita was the largest of all the airports I had seen, but apart from this fact I took very little notice of any of its other features. Later after travelling through Narita many times, I would begin to see the sheer scale of cleanliness, efficiency, and organisation that continued outwards to every part of Japan, a complete contrast to Tribhuvan airport in Kathmandu, where you spent most of your waiting time hustling for space and a moment's peace and quiet. Even the passport control officer seemed pleasant, though this was to be something of a rarity I later discovered as a seasoned traveller. He softened immediately when I stated I was here to learn karate and smiled pleasantly when I asked him to recommend a dojo to me. He wished me good luck and assured me I would find everything I was looking for in Tokyo.

I had not even the smallest clue of where I was heading to when I emerged from the doors of the arrival area at Narita Airport. In 1980 there were few people that spoke English and hardly any signs in English, but lucky for me I noticed a foreign guy walking towards the escalators with such confidence, I assumed he would know where to go. My assumption was correct, and he was kind enough to lead me to a bus that would take us to Tokyo and then on through the sprawling metropolis to a *ryokan* (guesthouse) in Ikebukuro where my search for a dojo would begin.

The owner of the guesthouse seemed taken by my small-town innocence and seemed very pleased to help me find a dojo. He scanned through the yellow pages, and the next day he took me to two dojos; the first I will purposely neglect to mention and then the second, the Japan Karate Association hombu (headquarters) dojo in Ebisu. I had no idea about the JKA and their karate, nor the reputation of some of the sensei who instructed there. I'd not even heard the name Nakayama-sensei, a name that later would become so important to me. But everything felt right about this dojo. From the moment I walked into the entrance I was hit with the sound of feet crashing to the floor as a class was in progress, I could feel my excitement getting the better of me and I wanted to rush in and see real Japanese karate for the first time. First I had to check in with the receptionist. Unfortunately, she spoke no English and with less than two days of Japanese life under my belt, the only word I knew was 'arigato' (thank you.) The limited exchange or words between us added to the confusion and I was certain she would not understand my reason for being here. Luckily a man approached from the rear of the office wearing a *dogi* (training uniform) and a heavily frayed black belt. He greeted me in strained English.

'Sensei, I've come to train in your dojo, is this okay?' I said innocently with a touch of nerves.

'Yes, this is okay.'

'Sensei, I want to gain my black belt in two months.'

'This is not possible,' he said with a wry smile.

I later learnt that this was Tanaka-sensei, who had won the All Japan Karate Championship two years in a row, a highly respected sensei at the JKA who would go on to teach me many things. The next day I enrolled in my first lesson at the JKA.

Training at the dojo every day and living at the guesthouse was not practical, so I managed to find an apartment with a Nepalese guy. His name was Bijoy, and he was here in Japan to study Japanese. Like all

Nepalese people, he loved to talk and ask many questions, even on subjects he had no familiarity with or interest in pursuing. It seemed he liked to absorb as much information as he could. We would often talk late into the night about our lives back home and the strange experiences that we met every day in Tokyo.

'Bijoy, the landlord was very mad with us today,' I once commented. Bijoy looked at me quizzically. 'Why Pemba?'

'He was crazy mad; he kept saying, "No pet, no pet",' I continued. 'I told him we don't have a pet, but he kept saying, "Cat, you have cat," and looking into our apartment.'

'That's crazy Pemba; we can't afford to keep ourselves, let alone a cat.'

'That's true, and I told him so, but he waved this in front of me,' I said, brandishing the offending object.

'An empty can?" ventured Bijoy.

'Yes. He's been going through our garbage,' I explained. Later I discovered this to be a common trait with landlords and neighbours, as they made sure we followed the strict separation and recycling rules that hadn't long come into place in Japanese society.

'I've been eating this for almost a week because it's the cheapest meat in the supermarket, and it's cheap for a reason Bijoy,' I said, hinting at my recent revelation.

'A reason?' Bijoy asked, curiously.

'Yes,' I said. 'It's cat food.'

Bijoy laughed for hours that day, and for the rest of the week every time he met my eyes he smirked and made cat noises, pushing his lips together and making that friendly sound we often-use to greet the neighbourhood cats. His playful mocking didn't stop there as it seemed my experiences in those first six months would provide a wealth of entertainment for Bijoy. Another particular favourite of his was my experience at our local *sento*.

A *sento* is a public bathing house found in every community; a tradition that has been around for over 400 years. The construction boom after the war saw to it that houses were built quickly and affordably, so baths were left out. This further cemented the tradition of bathing with neighbours for many years to come, and provided a relaxing and sociable atmosphere that continues even today. Naturally the baths were gender-segregated, but it took a little time for me to feel relaxed being naked in front of so many men. With nakedness, however, it seemed barriers were lowered and people would chat very openly and comfortably with each other. In those days, I didn't know enough Japanese to join in these conversations and because I was foreign, some people avoided eye contact or any kind of interaction with me. Perhaps it was for this reason that I spent almost a month washing my hair and body with washing-up liquid, another ill-gotten purchase from my local supermarket that stocked only Japanese goods labelled in *kanji* (Chinese characters). In my state of undress I was left feeling very embarrassed and stupid when a kindly Japanese gentleman, ferociously scrubbing himself next to me, raised his head with a smile and gestured at the bottle I was squeezing with one hand and preparing to lather into my body and hair with the other.

'Nan de? Are?' the man asked.

'Errr, chotto wakaranai,' I said, indicating that I didn't understand him.

'Dishu,' he said, leaning further forward and tapping the bottle, 'washu dishu only!'

Bijoy was not only amused by the many stories that paved my path as I made my way through the first six months of my Tokyo life, he was also interested in my enthusiasm for karate and his constant questions helped me clarify many things in my mind.

'What is the karate?' Bijoy asked with his usual inquisitive tone.

'It means empty hand. It is a form of self-defence that originated in Okinawa. It was brought to Japan by a famous karate sensei called Gichin Funakoshi in the early 20th century.'

'So, no nunchukas or throwing stars.' Bijoy had made no secret of his love for kung-fu movies.

'*Kara* means "empty", so only your hands and feet are used. In Okinawa it was forbidden to own a weapon, even a blunt display sword. The Okinawans had to develop a system that allowed them to protect themselves without using weapons. *Te*, means "hand", so karate translates as empty hand.'

The description seemed to satisfy Bijoy and his thirst for knowledge, but as the years rolled by I learnt more about the route of karate and learned that there was a much greater meaning to karate than just 'empty hand'.

I learned that the history was complex and somewhat refuted by many Japanese scholars, but it seemed logical that an empty handed system of defence would be born out of a prohibition of weapons. The first prohibition of weapons came when the Ryukyu, the three islands that now make up Okinawa, were forcibly changed from being independent states to a united kingdom under Sho Hashi (1372-1439), a dominion lord who became the first king of the Ryukyu kingdom. Immediately upon taking control of these islands, Sho Hashi set up a non-military government and prohibited the ownership of any weapons. This peace lasted for two centuries until they were attacked by the Shimizu who were the military governors in southern Kyushu, the third largest and most southern of the islands that make up Japan. The formidable Satsuma samurai, sent by the Shimazu from Kyushu, were surprised by the force of resistance from the previously peaceful islands, but nonetheless took control and reissued the ban on owning weapons in Ryukyu. The second ban was more thorough, across the general populace and upper classes, and it's thought by some historians that karate owes its creation to the second ban as it further fuelled the Ryukyu's desire to invent a means of unarmed combat.

The geographical position of the islands of Ryukyu also had great significance on the formation of karate since they were close to China. Trade between the two regions had flourished and it's believed that other exchanges were made such as the sharing of fighting arts. Chinese *kenpo*, translated as 'fist method' was most probably adapted and incorporated into the empty- handed art that was being developed in what is now called Okinawa. Around this period, this empty handed art became known under two names, Okinawa-te and To-de. Both these fighting forms embodied some of the Chinese ideals of combat that later became part of karate.

People often ask how long karate has been around, and if you follow the interpretation that its roots are found in Chinese fighting arts, then karate has been around for thousands of years. In fact, if you take it by its literal meaning, 'empty hand combat', then it's been around since one caveman threw his fist out in anger at another, though artistic impressions of this period would have us believe that it wasn't long before they discovered the club!

Scholars maintain that Chinese martial arts stretches back over 6,000 years. However, a more refined approach to combat can be traced back to the Chou dynasty (1027 BC) where under the efforts of three men, Ta Shang Lao-ch'un, Ta-yi Chen-jen and Yuan Shih-t'ien, systematised combat under the Three Primitive Schools of martial arts. These schools developed their skills throughout the ages with significant development during the Yuan (1279-1368), Ming (1368-1644) and Ch'ing (1644-19-12) dynasties where two prominent styles emerged: Shang Wu and Shaolin. Both styles became popular in China towards the end of the Ch'ing dynasty, with Shang Wu founded by Chang-san Feng placing greater emphasis on the development of *ch'i*, the mystical force that emulates from the *tanden* (just below the navel) often referred to as *ki* energy in Japanese. Off-shoots from this style continue to gain popularity even in the West, such as T'ai ch'i and Hsing-i.

The Shaolin style is better known in the West thanks to the enthusiasm of the Chinese and
Hong Kong film industry. The Shaolin style was founded by Ta-mo Lao-tsu (more commonly known as Bodhidharma) and praised for bringing Buddhism from India to China and subsequently most of Asia. Legend has it, that upon taking up a teaching role at the Shaolin monastery at the invitation of Emperor Hsiao Ming, under extreme training conditions he preceded to exhaust his students to the point of collapse. He felt that the spirit and flesh are one, so in order to reach spiritual enlightenment you had to push the boundaries of your physical being as well. Upon his students collapse he would discipline them and tell them that they would rise early tomorrow and repeat the extreme training until both their mind and body were strengthened according to the Ekikin and Senzui sutras. Ekikin, in kanji is made up of the characters 'eki,' meaning change and 'kin,' meaning muscles and combined refers to the disciplined toughening

of the body. Senzui, refers to 'washing away the dust of the mind' to uncover its true light. Bodhidharma believed that by following these two sutras strengthened the will to pursue a spiritual path and would develop an energy, known as ch'i (or ki, in Japanese) that could move mountains.

Both styles have recognisable traits that are now found in modern day karate. Shang Wu was admired for its explosive attacking techniques, with the body remaining as relaxed as possible until the moment of impact. The Shaolin style stressed the practical application of hand and foot techniques, both thrusting and snapping techniques. It's thought that both these styles found their way to the islands of Ryukyu and played a large part on the Okinawan styles of empty-handed combat.

Finally, in the Meiji period (1868-1912) the ban on weapons was lifted, but just before this happened, a small and sickly boy by the name of Gichin Funakoshi made his secretive start to an art that would go on to consume his life.

(In Darjeeling with my family before I left for Japan)

Chapter 3 The Reality

We all experience reality checks in life, but the one I first experienced when I enrolled for my first karate lesson at the Ebisu dojo came as a great shock to me. In my advancing years now, I often wonder what the outcome of my life would have been if I'd walked into the JKA dojo and been the best there, after all, I was the best at my dojo in Darjeeling, so why not here in Japan. Would I have been so enthused to train so hard over the next 40 years of my life? The answer of course, is 'no'.

Reality checks are therefore valuable, and on that first day in the Ebisu dojo, my immediate reactions of disappointment and despair when comparing my karate skill to those around me were those of a young and naïve man. It almost felt that all those hours, days, months and years of karate training in Darjeeling were in vain. I was wearing a white belt and even that seemed like a generous grade! My hopes and dreams of achieving my black belt in a few months were quashed on that hard wooden floor, faced with the instruction of Ueki-sensei and the students beside me who were faster, stronger and very noticeably technically superior.

The lesson had started well; while stretching for the first ten minutes I noticed no difference in my flexibility compared to the other students. I'd almost go as far as saying that I was one of the most flexible, aside from the sensei present in the class that day. Even if stretching lulled me into a false sense of security, it did give me a chance to glance around the dojo and take in the full atmosphere of the place. There was of course a large wooden floor, a small mirror-lined section wall near the entrance, a line of eight *makiwara* (a fixed vertical plank of wood used to develop punches and strikes) lining another wall. The central feature of the dojo was of course the 'kamidana', a small shrine to honour the living spirit that exists in everything. To the left of the *kamidana* was a picture of Funakoshi-sensei, and to the right of that a picture of Nakayama-sensei. On the same wall there was also a Japanese flag, officially known as the *Nisshoki* (sun mark) flag, though it's also known as the *Hinomaru*, or 'sun disc' flag, and a large scroll with beautiful kanji on it, which I later came to know as the 'dojo kun', or literally 'dojo rules'. But what struck me more than the features that made up this famous dojo was the atmosphere: an air of excitement mixed with fear hung in the air, you could sense that thousands of hours of blood, sweat and hidden tears had been shed here. The aura was almost overpowering on that first day, but years later I would learn to use that aura to drive me through some of the hardest days of my life.

Stretching was followed by first of the three main components of training, *kihon* (basics). This is where my world began to fall apart. Immediately one of the sensei descended upon me, moving my foot to adjust my stance, pulling my hips this way and that way, realigning my arm so my fists pointed clearly at either the *jodan* (face) or *chudan* (stomach) target. As I moved forward, a hand was thrust into my lower back to drive me along with the rest of the class. It felt like I was an invalid and being carried through the class like some helpless individual. Then came the kicks, an area in which I'd always felt confident. My kicks seemed to keep up with the rest of the class, but the sensei kept gesturing to his own stance and then raising his knee and smacking with both hands onto his backside to indicate that the hips somehow needed to be involved in the kick.

Then came the crushing blow as we embarked on some *kata* (forms), the second component of training. The *heian kata* I'd learnt back home had a similar inverted 'H' pattern but the similarities stopped there. It turned out to be one hell of a reality check, and as I recalled the events to Bijoy later that evening I went to sleep wondering if I would return to the dojo the next day.

With every new day brings renewed hope, so I decided to return to the dojo. The feeling of being below standard continued for the first month, and to combat this feeling I increased my training to every day (except Sunday, as the dojo was closed) and I also began training twice a day, an hour in the morning and then an hour in the evening. Slowly my techniques began to improve and I began to keep up with the other white belts and lower grades. Less attention was directed at me by the sensei, so I could only assume that my techniques were beginning to fall into line with the high standards of the JKA, at least for white belt level.

Unlike the first reality check, which happened all at once, the second reality check came to me slowly over those months. I had been training in karate for almost nine years before I decided to come to Japan. My instructor in Darjeeling wore a black belt but to this day I'm not sure if he was officially qualified; I now believe that much of what he taught he had tried to learn from books. I wasn't even completely clear which sensei he had trained under. Nevertheless, the classes in Darjeeling were quite free in terms of techniques and we often practiced some very impressive jumping and spinning kicks, much like you see now in Hollywood films. They looked very good, and from these acrobatic feats I assessed my own karate to be of a high standard; the higher I could kick, the higher my ability in karate. However, during my first six-month stint at the JKA, my feet never left the floor. I never spun, and I never tried to kick higher than my own head. I assumed that coming to Japan, the birthplace of karate, that I would be learning some amazing, elaborate, possibly secret techniques. But in reality we stuck religiously to basic methods. It was through the devoted study of the basics that I began to realise that instead of the elaborate, simplicity was king; instead of secrets, everything was broken down for the eye to see. I began to mature and appreciate even the most basic of movements.

After a few months I began to know the other students, not so much in their personalities because I had yet to understand the language, but I began to know their style of karate and how they performed in *kata* or *kumite* (sparring, the third major component of training). One student that impressed me was Okada-san; he was a brown belt and seemed to have a good skill in both *kata* and *kumite*. We would often spar and I remember being caught quite heavily by a *mawashi geri* (roundhouse kick) to the nose. I admired his skill and I used his level as a goal to attain and a yard stick against which to measure myself. Of course I wanted to be as good as Tanaka-sensei or Abe-sensei, but I'd already had two reality checks since joining the dojo and I didn't need a third.

Once I learnt more about the evolution of the *shotokan* style, I began to realise what an impossible task I had originally set for myself. As I mentioned earlier, much of the early history of karate is still contested by some academics, especially in regards to how much came from China and even further back, how much came from India. With so much secrecy surrounding *shotokan* karate and its early days in Okinawa, and the fact that little was recorded in writing, it's easy to understand why so much is contestable. What is clear, however, is how this beautiful art came to find its way to the mainland of Japan.

Gichin Funakoshi was born prematurely in Okinawa in 1868, at the start of the Meiji Restoration. He was born to a family of minor officials who began to worry seriously about his sickly nature and weak constitution. In fact, his family over compensated with love and affection as they truly believed that the young Funakoshi would not live very long. When he surprised them by living long enough to make it to primary school, he made friends with the son of a great karate master, Master

Azato. His grandparents made a request to Master Azato that their grandson could train with him in order to improve his health. In those days, Master Azato wasn't taking students due to the clandestine nature of training that characterised the era, but was happy to receive young Funakoshi at his house for private instruction in secret. What began as a remedy to improve the young Funakoshi's health, became a routine of training late into the night under a silvery moon and dim lantern where Master Azato would position himself whilst giving instruction, blossomed into a lifelong devotion to karate. It's easy to understand why this interest was sparked. In just over two years, young Funakoshi's health improved dramatically and he was no longer the weak and sickly boy he had been. Furthermore, his love for karate had grown so steadily that he began contemplating making karate a way of life.

Master Azato was also great friends with another local karate master, Master Itosu, and when the young Funakoshi began to show talent for karate, Master Azato insisted he also train with Master Itosu to broaden his understanding of karate. They both became his regular teachers but continued to insist he take instruction from other great masters when he could; back then, it seemed there were no issues of loyalty to one teacher or style.

Sometimes it's easy to see a path that emerges through someone's life when you're given enough time to reflect on it, though it's also easy to fit a path for that person towards your own romanticised inclinations. Funakoshi-sensei had chosen to become a doctor, and passed the exam to attend a prestigious medical school in Tokyo. However, he never became a doctor as at the time he refused to cut his topknot (a traditional Japanese hairstyle) which under the new Meji government was seen as an unnecessary fixation with the past. The new government had passed edicts in which men would not be allowed to enter certain institutions if they persisted on wearing their hair in this manner. At the time, Funakoshi-sensei, not wishing to offend his family, refused the wishes of the new Meji government, and therefore wasn't allowed to attend the medical school. Ironically, several years later he succumbed to these forced changes and cut it off so he could pursue a career in teaching. It would seem that the timing and chain of events guided Funakoshi-sensei to become a teacher; had he become a doctor, it's logical to surmise that karate would exist today in a very different form.

It was during Funakoshi's career as a teacher, and the subsequent lifting of the ban on practicing martial arts, that he was able to develop karate into the school system of Okinawa where it began to draw much attention from wider Japanese society, especially from military leaders who would often visit the island on manoeuvres. As the young students that Funakoshi taught matured and joined universities, the military and other notable institutions, it became apparent that these young men were physically and spiritually more impressive and that karate was responsible for this. Soon Funakoshi-sensei was invited to Tokyo to demonstrate karate and even gave a demonstration to the great judo master, Jigo Kano at the Budokan, where it was warmly received. Soon it was being taught to the military, schools and some companies and apart from the Second World War it has continued to develop at pace thanks to the passion, drive and devotion of Funakoshi-sensei.

Passion, drive and devotion was all around me when I trained at the JKA, from the students that came just a few times a week due to their heavy work schedules, to the students that came every day like me, and of course, all the instructors that taught at the dojo. They all understood how karate had impacted their lives and made improvements to both their physical and mental wellbeing.

Outside of the dojo, my time was taken up washing dishes at a local restaurant owned by an Indian man. I had little concern with learning the language, after all, I was only here for a short time to gain my black belt and then leave. The language barrier in the dojo didn't seem to matter, as a lot of what I learnt was through visual explanation and I, in such awe of the technical level, concentrated on imitating the technique as best as I could, instead of questioning things. Apart from encountering difficulty with *kanji*, especially when making food and shampoo purchases, I could get by on a daily basis without too much trouble. I had worked out a simple system for dealing with the trains and network of stations. Travelling from my apartment to the dojo I used the Yamanote line, a train line popular with commuters as it circled the entire central area of Tokyo. It did this with such reliability and efficiency, but the only trouble was that at the time every station looked relatively the same, and none of the signage was in English, so instead of trying to memorise the kanji, I memorised that there were eight stations between Ikebukuro and Ebisu, and so as long as I counted correctly and didn't fall asleep, I was generally on time for training.

There was little in the way of excitement in those first six months, and little interaction with the locals apart from in the dojo. I had no money to go out drinking, nor eat in nice restaurants and hadn't had the opportunity to make many friends. I did make one friend who would kindly allow me to watch his TV. This was a big thing for me as back home no one in my town had a TV and even though I couldn't understand the words that were being spoken, the moving images were very satisfying, allowing me to view a whole variety of different places, people and of course food.

The Japanese are fanatical about their food, and it seemed that a lot of air-time was devoted to food programs. You could even say there was a certain eroticism with how they filmed food programs; zooming in for a close ups, filming celebrities eating and responding with an obligatory exclamation of *'Oishii!'* ('Delicious!'), it was a real passion and there seemed to be a huge sense of pride surrounding Japanese rice. Naturally, I grew very fond of Japanese food, but couldn't afford to enjoy it to the fullest during the first six months.

The only TV program I understood and really enjoyed was late on Saturday nights, the music show *Best Hit USA*. It almost became the highlight of my week, though sometimes my friend would say he needed to sleep, so I often missed out on this treat. In truth, I longed for home, to be with my mother, brothers and sister, and of course I missed the admiration and flattery that the townsfolk had begun to shower me with, both for my volunteer work and my karate skills. In the village I was a big fish in a small pond; over here in Japan, I was a small fish in a big pond, and judging by the response of many of my sensei, I didn't swim so well.

My dream of achieving a black belt had taken several reality checks, and it seemed the only thing to do was to return home and continue supporting my family, maybe take a course and prepare for my future job. I could at least say that I came to Japan, that I left my town and had some experience in a foreign country; people would respect me enough for that.

(Japan Karate Association (JKA) Hombu Dojo, Ebisu, Tokyo)

(Masatoshi Nakayama, April 13th 1913- April 15th 1987, Founder and Chief Instructor of the JKA)

Chapter 4 Guilt

Something changes when you leave home; your eyes are never quite the same again. They've seen things, things that go beyond the horizons of home. I'd only been away six months and it seemed the longest part of my trip was taking four flights to get home! But, I felt different inside.

Once again it seemed simple, I would return home, enjoy the warm reception, answer a few questions about Japan and explain that the standard of karate made it impossible to gain a black belt in such a short time. Things would go back to normal, minus burying the dead.

What I'd failed to realise is that by going to Japan I was not only carrying the hopes and dreams that were my own, but also those of my town. There was a genuine look of disappointment on the face of each person who welcomed me home and discovered that I hadn't achieved my black belt. While, courtesy of the reality checks I experienced, I understood how impossible it would be for anyone to gain a black belt in such a short space of time. Many of my family, friends and townsfolk didn't buy into this reason. It seemed I had inadvertently made another contract, and with this contract unfulfilled I was paying a heavy price in guilt and regret.

I learned that failure has a double edged sword; you have to live with the sharp stab of your own regret and disappointment and then look into the eyes of those that believed in you and live with theirs. Pride of course plays its part and in my advancing years I've seen pride and regret eat a man up. Eventually you can put this regret to sleep, but it's only sleeping. It will awaken to cause you pain later. At this time I had no understanding of these things, but for three months I felt the sharpness of that doubled edged sword. And what of my family's pride; I'm sure, while I was away in Japan getting my black belt, my mother walked the town with her head held higher, maybe my brothers boasted on my behalf and my sister felt flattered when someone asked how Pemba was getting on. The promises I'd made to myself, to them, the townsfolk, and of course, Kangchenjunga were becoming too much to bear.

Before I left for my trip to Japan I visited my favourite mountain, the third highest mountain in the world and prayed for my success and vowed to not look at the mountain again until I reached my goal of black belt. Making such a vow and then returning to Darjeeling was foolhardy, since Kangchenjunga is only 300 meters lower than Mount Everest and visible from almost every angle of our town. The townsfolk must have thought I had some strange affliction as I tried to navigate the town without staring directly at Kangchenjunga. I'd also made this prayer at my favourite tea garden and in front of my favourite pine tree that I'd loved since childhood.

Growing up surrounded by the Himalayas and beautiful nature, you familiarise yourself by choosing favourite landmarks and I had come to love Kangchenjunga, the tea garden and a tall pine tree as if they were my own. We didn't have toys growing up, instead we had the greatest gifts from nature and I was happy to claim them as my own. The mountain, the tea garden and the pine tree belonged to me and I came to treasure them as though they were part of my family. Making a promise like that to Kangchenjunga was like promising my own grandfather that I'd bring him back a gift from my trip and then turning up empty handed. I'd made a binding contract with myself, my family, friends, the townsfolk and the most noticeable mountain range in the world. It was too much to bear.

I tried hard to push this contractual obligation from my mind by enrolling in a college course so I could finish my education that I had neglected to do after my father passed away. It seemed to add further salt to my wounds when I was offered a very prestigious and well paid job, teaching karate at a private school in Darjeeling. The salary was three times the local average and seemed too big a reward for not gaining my black belt. The school was obviously familiar with the positive effects that karate would provide the future elite that studied there, they were even willing to accept me, a mere sixth *kyu* (green belt grade), the grade I'd managed to achieve after six months at the JKA, a grade that was six grades off a *shodan* (black belt), as their head instructor. Upon taking the position I immediately developed mixed feelings. I remember how I felt attending a lunch reception to welcome new students and teachers. As well as feeling uncomfortable by the attire I had to wear, I felt like a complete fraud as I stood amongst the other professors and lapped up the praise that comes from reaching such a high level of academic attainment. How could I possibly fit in, if my area of expertise was karate and I was here to teach it to the men of the future? Did having a sixth *kyu* from the JKA really warrant my appointment among these academic scholars? It was no longer a case of feeling like a big fish in a small pond, the feeling was more like being a fish out of water.

Of course my memories of training at the JKA also played heavily on my mind. I tried hard to continue my training at my old dojo and even practicing alone at the volunteer centre but I just didn't feel I was doing my karate justice. I became disheartened, depressed and carried with me everywhere, that uneasy feeling that comes when you're not sure which direction your life is going. Maybe in time these feelings would go away and my mind would return to normal, but my character wouldn't allow these thoughts to go away so I had little choice, for the sake of my sanity, to return to Japan and fulfil the contract completely.

(Some of the townsfolk in Darjeeling)

Chapter 5 The First Peak

I'd managed to find a more direct flight this time and only had to endure three flights, instead of four. I arrived back in Japan early in the morning and while I hadn't slept well on the plane, I was wide awake and hungry for success. The image of Kangchenjunga firmly etched in my mind as a reminder not to fail this time. I later realised the philosophical significance of linking my goal to that of my beloved mountain. Staring up at the peak of a huge mountain, knowing that you have to climb it to succeed in your journey can be quite disheartening and this was true of my quest for the black belt. However, once you observe the stages that need to be traversed on your journey to the summit and you begin to reach the first stage and then the next, everything becomes a little more manageable and achievable. I'd started my second run at the JKA *hombu dojo* with a green belt round my waist, so I could take confidence that I had at least climbed a few rungs and the peak looked a little more achievable.

I'd also managed to secure my old room again, though Bijoy had moved on, thankfully taking his cat noises with him. I also found work at a book factory providing me with money to eat, but unfortunately that meant I could only train the evening sessions at the dojo. So for the first few months I trained two, sometimes three hours a day at the dojo. My three months absence hadn't been noticed and everyone treated me as though I'd never left.

In those days, before politics and the ensuing split, the JKA *hombu dojo* had a very large membership and it was common to see over a hundred students at any time, attending the three or four classes that were scheduled each night. There was a separate children and women's class, and of course there was an instructor's class. I attended the regular classes for all grades and these were usually full. With the success of many of the sensei and some students on the tournament circuit, it was easy to see why the JKA *hombu dojo* was regarded as the largest and most famous karate dojo in the world.

After the Second World War, Japan was a country in devastation, though that devastation is a testament to the Japanese resolve that over the next forty years, they rebuilt themselves into one of the most economically advanced nations in the world. This progress was also replicated in the area of karate. Funakoshi-sensei had seen his first *hombu dojo* in Tokyo flattened by bombs and more sadly many of his promising students fail to return from the war. It's a measure of his devotion to karate that instead of returning to Okinawa to be with his family, he remained in Tokyo to continue developing karate. He rebuilt his dojo and continued to teach at various institutions throughout Tokyo, including the famous Takushoku University. Prior to the war, he had begun to develop some strong students at this university, in fact this university would go on to produce some of the finest *karateka* in the world.

It was at Takushoku University that he began to teach a young man called Masatoshi Nakayama, who ironically arrived at the dojo to take a kendo class but had misread the schedule and found himself watching and becoming drawn to karate. His descendants came from a *budo* background and taught *kenjutsu* and his father practiced judo, so it was quite natural for the young Nakayama to pursue some form of *budo* training at university. It's lucky for the karate world that in those days he was not very good at reading schedules!

Nakayama-sensei graduated Takushoku University with his *shodan* and a degree in Chinese language and became an interpreter in China during Japanese occupation. He returned to Japan after the war and became more and more involved in the development of *shotokan* karate. Along with his teacher, Gichin Funakoshi and other notable students such as Isao Obata and Hidetaka Nishiyama they formed the Japan Karate Association in 1949. Gichin Funakoshi was around eighty years old by then so became the head of the JKA whilst Nakayama was appointed chief instructor. Gigo Funakoshi who followed his father to Tokyo at the age of seventeen also did much for the development of modern karate, especially in regards to kicks, lower stances and the use of the hips when blocking. Sadly Gigo died at the age of thirty-nine from tuberculosis during the tough conditions that proceeded the war and alas was to contribute no more to the development of *shotokan* karate. When Funakoshi sensei died in 1957 some of his senior students, upset by the funeral arrangements and the general direction of the JKA, decided to form their own organisations that they claimed followed Funakoshi's ideals more closely. Nakayama-sensei continued to develop karate throughout Japan and into the rest of the world and his success was clear when *shotokan* students began to dominate the tournament circuit during the 50s and 60s.

I respected and understood how the JKA emerged and felt even more devoted to training and was content, at least for the time being, to live a very simple and frugal life. I found that in order to maximise my training time, I'd work full time for a couple of months, only attending the dojo in the evening and then with the money I saved, I'd quit my job and use it to support me for the next few months to have the freedom to attend all the classes I could; daytime and evening. This certainly improved my level in karate but also led me to experience real hunger for the first time.

In order to save money from working I would invest wisely in packs of thirty five yen noodles. I would bulk buy and spend up to five-thousand yen at once to ensure I had plenty of food to keep me going. That amounted to a lot of noodles, and often the supermarket would bring me a box from the store room instead of trying to take them off the shelf. Over the next nine months my diet consisted of noodles, natto (fermented soybeans) and on special occasions a small helping of chicken. Having no refrigerator limited my options, and I had no rice cooker and only the means to boil one pot. Finding a job was not always easy and often I would run out of food before I had money coming in. I remember going two or three days with just water to sustain me. This made training even more challenging and often by the third day I would break into a fever. On one particular occasion I had struggled to sleep after three days of just water. I was feverish and in a real daze. I managed to muster the energy to walk to Ikebukuro, a large city area in north-west Tokyo, where there were several big department stores with large food departments. This upmarket food hall was made up of small bakeries, delicatessen, bento (lunch box) sellers and wine merchants, and many of the counters offered a selection of sample food to entice customers to buy. I found myself relying on these enticing nibbles to nourish myself during these hard times. I would take a small slice of cheese and eat it slowly and with measured control trying desperately hard to mask the fact that I was starving. I would nod and say 'Oishii,' (delicious) the obligatory response when eating food. Sometimes my hunger got the better of me and I would ashamedly return to the same counter for seconds. Thanks to Japanese politeness this didn't pose too much trouble but my pride was severely damaged by the reproach in their gaze.

So my life went like this for almost a year. Training every day, working every couple of months, eating just noodles and *natto*, and occasionally starving for a few days. Whenever things felt really tough, I would think of Kangchenjunga, the tea garden or the pine tree and this drove me to train harder and harder. I also reflected on the legend of Bodhidharma and how he would drive his students to exhaustion to help them reach spiritual enlightenment, though at this young age, the only enlightenment I received was to understand fully the scope and beauty of the thirty-five yen pack of noodles! Then, finally, the day came to take my black belt grading.

Of course I wasn't alone when I took my grading. In fact I would hazard a guess that about a hundred other students were taking their dan grading as well. They had come from all over Japan and some from abroad, and the grading panel consisted of many senior and junior senseis. I remember seeing Tanaka-sensei, Ueiki-sensei, Shoji-sensei, Asai-sensei, Abe-sensei, and Yahara and Osaka who were both junior *sensei* in those days.

I was very fortunate to be taking my grading that day, as JKA rules stated that I must be training karate at the JKA for a minimum of two years before I could take *shodan*. Including my three month break to return home, I'd only been training with the JKA for a year and half and many of the sensei informed me that I was not eligible to take this grading. I nervously approached Tanaka-sensei and with my improved Japanese skill I explained that I had been studying karate for almost ten years and felt ready to take my *shodan*. I don't know whether Tanaka-sensei remembered our first meeting at the dojo reception when I proclaimed that I wanted my black belt in two months and he had smiled wryly and said 'This is not possible,' but he approved my application to take *shodan*.

When the results were posted on the dojo wall later that week my heart leapt with joy when I saw my name under the group marked 'passed.' I celebrated with chicken that night, and slept with a smile on my face knowing that I could now face Kangchenjunga, the tea garden and the pine tree.

At the end of the week, we had a graduation ceremony to celebrate our new grades and tradition had it that our sempai (senior) would fight us very strongly in *kumite*, many students getting *bloodied* and beaten quite badly, though I know now that this level of beating was very soft compared to what I would receive later on in my karate career. As far as I could tell, this was done as a reminder to us that the journey was far from over, that wearing a black belt meant a new beginning, not an end to study, unlike most graduation events, like college or university. While receiving a beating at what was supposed to be a celebration, I didn't really appreciate this philosophical point, that karate was a journey with stages and this journey never ends, but I appreciate it now. It saddens me, now as an instructor, at how many students of karate end their practice when they reach *shodan*, like it's some kind of final destination, as though there are no longer anymore peaks to climb.

During the 'celebrations' I also received a bloodied nose, but not as bad as other students. My *kumite* skills over the past few months had begun to develop quite well, well enough to attract the attention of the strongest group of students known as *kushikai*. In such a large organisation such as the JKA it was common for inner groups to form and often these groups would represent as a team at many of the tournaments around Japan.

For me, being accepted into *kushikai* group was a very happy occasion and finally allowed me to bond closely with the Japanese. Alcohol seemed to be a very good bonding agent and for the first time, I began to enjoy the bars and nightlife that Tokyo had to offer. I was proud to be part of the strongest group in the dojo and their strength in the dojo was matched by their drinking prowess. Like many groups there was a hierarchy and the head of our group was part of an even more formidable group, the *yakuza* (Japanese mafia.) He was a very kind and generous man and would often treat the whole group to nights out, though I use the term 'night' very loosely as the drinking sessions would often go on until the early morning leaving me just a few hours before I would start training at the dojo. I quickly learned that training under the effects of alcohol was as bad as training without having eaten for several days.

We began to attend many tournaments as a group around the Tokyo area. Slowly I began to feel my confidence growing. At a tournament in Shibuya, I was about to fight another opponent and there was a little fuss made by my senior as to who I was fighting. I asked who the guy was and they replied, 'no one special.' They had decided not to tell me that he was the Wado Ryu world champion. Neglecting to tell me this probably benefited me, as I went into the fight with no expectations and managed to score a point against him when he tried to sweep me with *ashi barai* (foot sweep) and I lifted my foot in time to swing round and catch him with *uraken uchi* (back fist strike). Unfortunately, after that earlier point, the referring decisions tended to go against me and I lost the fight.

My desire to compete grew stronger and in 1985, I entered my first major world tournament, the Shoto World Cup, and for the first time attended the famous Budokan. The same Budokan that Funakoshi-sensei visited to demonstrate his karate for the famous judo master Jigo Kano, all those years ago. The Budokan was originally built for the 1964 Olympic judo tournament, but had now become the spiritual home for many martial arts. With over fourteen-thousand seats, it had also become a very popular venue for concerts with many famous bands appearing there due to its good acoustics and octagonal shape which gave an exciting gladiatorial 'arena feel'. When I first stepped onto one of the side mats, it seemed like any other tournament, but when I made it through to the last sixteen in the *kata* tournament I saw the Budokan from a whole different perspective, from the centre stage, and it was terrifying!

I'd already lost in the third round at *kumite* to Yokomichi sempai, a respectable world champion, but as I progressed in the *kata* tournament, first demonstrating some of the heian kata (basic kata) and then on to the knock out rounds where one of four kata were selected for you out of *Bassai-dai*, *Kanku-dai*, *Jion* and *Empi*. I performed *Kanku-dai* which was good enough to put me through to the last sixteen. The last sixteen meant competing on the central mat, for everyone to see. During the final round I could choose my own *kata* and opted for *Bassai-dai*. I can remember performing this *kata* but the most vivid of that memory was the strange feeling I had, as though I was floating on the mat, unable to grip the mat and apply a strong finish to my techniques. I was awarded eleventh place, which was a satisfying result considering the line-up of talent on display at the Budokan that late-afternoon. Kawada went on to win both the *kata* and *kumite* tournament.

Over the years I became best in *kushikai* group. I even beat Okada in *kumite*, with whom I'd built up a healthy rivalry for many years and always aspired to be as good as in *kumite* and *kata*. It was now time to search for a new peak to climb. Fortunately, I'd been attending Osaka-sensei's *kata* class every Wednesday evening and had learned a lot from the great *kata* master. We would spend weeks and weeks on the same *kata* before moving on to the next one, so my *kata* began to improve very noticeably. I attended Osaka sensei's special *kata* class for four years without fail and I'll be forever grateful for the depth of learning I experienced under this great master. Thanks to Funakoshi-sensei's relentless campaign to develop and promote karate and the discovery of talented men like Nakayama-sensei, the JKA came into existence and I was able to develop, what had now become my life-long passion for karate.

I also began to develop a love for Japan itself and felt a great sense of achievement that I could now communicate quite well in Japanese. I hadn't *learned* to read Japanese, but English translations began to appear in the more central areas of Tokyo, especially station names. Sharing time with Japanese friends and watching Japanese TV, I began to understand more and more about this country I was now calling home. Of course, it drew some similarities with my own country, but on the whole, it was very different. There seemed to be a lot more emphasis on cooperation instead of confrontation and group participation for the good of the whole, as opposed to just self-interest. Group formation and hierarchy is common throughout Japanese society and it seems to work to the benefit of the country. Cooperation is key to getting things done, but to me, there always seemed such a heavy contrast in Japan with one set of people trying so hard to fit in, whilst another group were going to extremes to avoid group association. Sometimes on a Sunday afternoon, I would walk through Harajuku, a cosmopolitan area of Tokyo and note the extreme states of dress by many of the young people. You would see teenagers dressed in anything from bright pink fairy outfits to dark, gothic leather wear, though it occurred to me that instead of trying to repel the group mentality of dressing the same, unlike the millions of 'salary men' who wear the same dark suit and tie to work every day, they were actually conforming to another group, a group of the 'strangely dressed.' So it seemed that groups had been formed with the sole purpose of rejecting group mentality, which seemed a little ironic to me.

Being a foreigner in a new country allows you to observe things from a different perspective than the locals and it was natural to make comparisons to home, but the longer I stayed, the less I began to miss my home near the Himalayas. I of course missed nature, and would often jump on a train and venture out to one of the far off suburbs to get as close to nature as I could.

The train system always impressed me with its cleanliness and efficiency, though being squashed into a carriage during rush hour did give me some cause for complaint. The other thing that used to shock me were the reasons given for the train delays. In my own country, delays were often due to faulty trains and tracks, or a worker strike, but in Tokyo, it seemed quite common to hear that someone had jumped in front of a train. It shocked me when I discovered that Japan had one of the highest suicide rates in the world, for an industrialized country. I must have been under some kind of romantic illusion as to how well Tokyo operated as a city. It seemed so full of hustle and bustle, so much energy, enterprise and wealth, that I didn't initially observe the darker side to living in Japan. It shocked me to hear that the rail companies actually charged a fee to the grieving family whose loved one had caused such inconvenience and delay to the train system. It shocked me further to hear that the desperate souls wishing to take their lives were often angry at their family and would remove their shoes and leave them at the edge of the platform to signify that it was suicide and not a tragic accident, therefore not allowing their family to dispute the hefty fee they would receive.

It's difficult to understand why Japan has one of the highest suicide rates in the world. On the one hand, it's a very group and cultural driven society, but on the other, this strong sense of group belonging could alienate certain people and lead them to slip into hard states of depression and desperation. There is, of course, a historical element to suicide in Japanese culture, attached to the *bushido*, the code of the samurai. To avoid the shame of being captured by enemy soldiers, they would commit *seppuku* which involved using a small blade known as a *tanto* and following a strict ritual would slice across their abdomen from left to right causing disembowelment and death. The samurai would have to seek permission from their *daimyo* (feudal lords) to commit *seppuku*. If they had dishonoured the clan or committed a crime, they would be ordered to commit *seppuku*. Often a second, known as *kaishakunin* would be present to decapitate the head to ensure a quick and less painful death. It was of course a great honour to be called on as a second but this also required a high degree of skill as the aim was not to sever the head completely but allow enough skin to remain, allowing the head to fall forward and into an 'embraced' position with the torso. Forced *seppuku* was also used as a form of capital punishment but was abolished in 1873, after the Meiji Restoration. Since then it has been depicted in many films and was especially popular in many *kabuki* (traditional Japanese theatre) performances and though it is no longer a tradition that is still practiced, it has been known to be used occasionally, especially amongst high ranking officials and disgraced captains of industry. In fact, the last reported *seppuku* was in 2001. Historically, *seppuku* has been an elitist affair, reserved only for the samurai classes, but the history of the samurai and *seppuku* may have painted a romanticised picture for those tortured souls that continue to put a swift end to their life in modern Japan by stepping in front of a speeding train.

Stories of the samurai, the culture, along with my improving karate and grasp of the Japanese language, encouraged me to stay after I reached, what became my first peak, gaining my *shodan*. I felt as though I had only begun to scratch below this beautiful country with its strange culture and traditions. It was also clear to me that gaining my *shodan* had done nothing to end my quest in Japan, but instead brought me in to view of much larger peaks.

(*kushikai* team *kumite* at the JKA All Japan Tournament at the Budokan)

Chapter 6 *Kenshusei*

It was never my intention to take the *kenshusei* course, I'd trained as a regular student at the *hombu dojo* for six years and I'd seen those brave *kenshusei*, distraught looking characters, bandaged and bruised, moving anxiously around the dojo. I had just competed in my first major tournament, The Shoto World Cup, in 1985 and placed 'best eleven' in the kata and lost in the *kumite* to Yokomichi, a formidable opponent. Other students began to ask me, why don't you do the *kenshusei* course? Though I just fobbed it off with a laugh and a smile, inside I was thinking, 'Are you crazy? Have you seen the punishment those guys take?'

I hadn't been married long to my first wife, who was also a karate student, and it seemed that I had gone from one dish-washing or bar-tending job to another. This made me very self-conscious about my low status witnessed by my wife and the country that had now become my adopted home. My wife reminded me that I had come to Japan for karate and that I should take it as far as I can. She meant the *kenshusei*, of course. Eventually her logic, the coaxing of other students, and one too many dirty dishes got the better of me and I decided to apply to take the *kenshusei* course.

I was also drawn by the history of the course and some of the legends it had produced. Nakayama-sensei introduced the course in 1956. His aim was to produce a professional elite that could spread karate to every corner of the globe. Undoubtedly he achieved this, producing the likes of Hirokazu Kanazawa, Eiji Takaura and Takayuki Mikami in the first batch of graduates. Mikami-sensei went off to develop *shotokan* karate throughout the United States, and Kanazawa- sensei is still teaching all over the world even today. The first year of graduates wasn't just a fluke, as year after year, the course produced high calibre sensei, including the likes of Keinosuke Enoeda, Masaaki Ueki, Yahara and Kagawa sensei and many more.

The course evolved over the years and it now took three years to graduate if you entered as a regular student, and two years if entering as a graduate from an affiliated university. Before your application could be accepted you had to approach a senior sensei for their endorsement. I decided to approach Yahara-sensei as over the years he had taken a particular interest in my karate, teaching me many things. I was also, like many, in complete awe of his technical ability. He seemed to have a natural ability and moved his body perfectly when executing techniques. His performance of the *kata*, Unsu was breath-taking and hearing him punch the *makiwara* (a striking board) in the dojo sent shivers down the spine. He was also a successful businessman and had a large international following in both business and karate. He was extremely admirable, though known for having a quick temper. I approached him cautiously and he replied,

"Do you want to join the instructor classes or enrol on the instructor's course?"

"The course sensei," I replied with doubt featuring heavily in my voice.

"You do understand what the course entails?"

"Oss, sensei," I said, sounding a little less doubtful.

"Think about it for one month and then come back and see me," was his final stern response.

I felt relieved; I had prodded the tiger but stepped away unharmed and without loss of face. However, I didn't wait a month to make my second approach; after discussing it with my wife, I returned the next day and Yahara-sensei continued to treat my request with caution. As we approached Asai-sensei's office, he stopped me again at the door.

"Tamang, before we step through this door I'm giving you one last chance to escape. You can

walk away now and I will say nothing more about it, but if you walk through that door there is no going back. The next three years will be the hardest years of your life."

"Oss, I go sensei," trying my best to sound brave and mask my fear.

Asai -sensei seemed pleased to accept my application and said he would approach Nakayama -sensei on my behalf. It was a success and I was permitted to take the entrance examination. This consisted of a written paper and a test of *kumite* and *kata*. A few days later I received the results and was filled with both joy and fear. Joy at the prospect of completing the same course that all the respected sensei had completed in their youth and helped them rise to such greatness and fear of subjecting my body and without realising it then, my mind, to three years of torture.

When we started in April 1986, I was one of two recruits. The other was Yoko Nakamura who was already world *kata* champ with her performance of Unsu, and she became my *doki* (dojo partner), as we were both the same age, in fact at 26 years old we were regarded as the old timers of the group. We also joined Yasuo Hanzaki who was a student in his senior year, who went on to become a full time instructor at the JKA. On paper the course didn't look that bad, we were told to arrive one hour before our class at 10 am and prepare the dojo. This involved placing small wet towels around the dojo used to add grip on the slippery floor and also plenty of cloths for cleaning the dojo floor. I later discovered that this was very important for cleaning up certain spillages that would become common during our *kenshusei* training. We would also prepare tea for the sensei, which I became very fond of. Being in the small kitchen preparing the cups, tea and other things associated with making tea meant I was away from the dojo floor. The regular class finished at 10.30 am which left the dojo floor free for half an hour. This period before our class was a time the sensei's liked to warm up on one of the *kenshusei* and it was here that I first became acquainted with Kagawa-sensei's foot when he caught me perfectly with his trademark powerful *mawashi geri* (round house kick). It became common to feel dazed, bruised and exhausted even before the class had started, unless of course I was on tea duty!

The official class lasted for one or two hours and this was four days a week. However, there was always training around the classes, like the thirty minute warm-up time for the sensei, and if they enjoyed warming up, then they had an even greater thirst for warming down. Once we had finished meditating, reciting the *dojo kun*, and bowing, the class had officially finished, but this is when the real pain began. Sometimes you would find yourself sparring with a sensei for fifteen, twenty minutes and then as you stood there, dazed and bruised and desperately trying to catch your breath, another sensei would say, "TAMANG, let's go," and the fighting would continue until you were blooded, bruised and exhausted, until I fully understood why the *kenshusei* students I had seen all those years ago, limped around the dojo with an expression of absolute misery on their faces. It was a strange conundrum, you dreaded sparring with the sensei's but the dread seemed almost as unbearable when you were alone, stretching, practicing or trying to warm down, because this was the period when you were fair game and you wondered in fear which sensei would be next to say those fearful words, "TAMANG, let's go."

Having a woman for my *doki* proved to be a huge disadvantage; whilst she was a formidable karate student and I learned many things from her, the gender inequalities that inevitably existed meant the sensei's felt restrained from 'letting loose' their powerful arsenal of techniques, so it often felt like I was taking her punishment as well.

As I reflect with a great sense of happiness and pride on this period of my life, I recall being asked about the *kenshusei* course in an interview. The question was asked if in the three years of *kenshusei* and practicing *kumite* with all those famous sensei, did I ever get the upper hand and score a few points. After I stopped laughing, I confessed to the interviewer that I don't even recall landing one single punch or successful kick. It wasn't that I was terrible at *kumite*, after all, in my final year I became the 1988 Kuwait International Champion. It's just the level of these men was superhuman. Most of them had trained every day of their lives for 40-50 years. Watching the three of us fight with the sensei's was the equivalent of watching Mike Tyson in his heyday take on the towel boy! We were a desperate sight to see, though. One thing is for sure: my blocking, evading and running ability improved massively in those three years. As for my attacking and counter-attacking skills, they were left to develop on the other *kenshusei* and regular students. None of my suffering fellow students fared any better, and I'm sure, like me, they used to only dream of getting their own back and for once, surprising one of the sensei's. This of course changed during the years after my graduation and I found myself competing against the likes of Kagawa-sensei in world tournaments. Tournaments have strict rules in place to protect the competitors, so it was more than possible to score against them in open tournaments, but in the dojo during the *kenshusei* course, there was no chance and there was no referee to stop the fight if the contact got too heavy and it was this heaviness that was designed to toughen the inside as well as the outside.

They say the samurai didn't fear death in battle. In fact, it was an honour to die in such a way, that surviving a losing battle was shameful. Bushido, the way of the samurai was the ultimate code of disciplined training. Remnants of this code seemed very much alive in the *kenshusei* course. The constant brutality was devised to prepare our mind and body for real combat. People, not experienced in this level of brutality, when faced with an aggressive and possibly violent situation, can experience what is known as an 'adrenalin dump'. This is when all of your strength and courage leaves your body momentarily as your mind comes to terms with an extreme level of fear. It's also described as the 'rabbit in the headlights' effect, when a rabbit crossing a road is met with headlights and instead of bouncing away safely, freezes in its tracks and the inevitable happens. The rabbit is killed by shock and inaction. I could relate to this during the first few months of fighting the likes of Yahara and Kagawa-sensei, but of course, the more accustomed to the 'headlights' I became, the more I began to manage my fear and react without delay, and the less I got 'run over'!

On occasion though, I did lose my concentration enough to receive many injuries. I remember when Yahara-sensei caught me in the face with a perfectly executed kick and my nose swelled up. The following day, Abe-sensei asked me what happened, so I told him. Then came those fearful words, 'Tamang, let's go,' and once again, appearing from what seemed like nowhere, his foot caught me on the side of the face and left a bruise under my eye. Tanaka-sensei followed up the next day with the same question and yet another bruise to my face. I was so black and blue that when I arrived that evening at my bar job, my boss refused to have me work, saying that I would scare the customers away. I lost around ten thousand yen waiting for my injuries to heal. I tell this story with some affection now as I don't believe there was a conspiracy to seriously injure me, after all I was never hospitalised during those three years. It was more a 'testing of my mettle' in true *budo* spirit. Years later I would draw on this spirit when in trouble on the streets and bars of India and Nepal.

The fear of physical confrontation had been extinguished during those three years of *kenshusei*, so to face several drunken men in a bar seemed far less intimidating than standing in front of Tanaka-sensei when he's about to apply his artistic skills to my face.

The physical injuries were harsh during those years and I suffered a broken nose six times. Often the sensei's lined up and one by one and we had to go along the line and fight them all. Of course, after the first fight, you were already battered, bruised and exhausted and I would look to my right and see that I still had Yahara, Tanaka, Kagawa and Abe-sensei still left to fight. I can't even begin to describe the extreme feeling of hopelessness that runs through your mind at that point. It wasn't uncommon for us to drop to our knees in complete resignation, though the nearest sensei would always grab us by the belt and wrench us back to our feet and the fighting would continue. It wasn't just an extreme physical challenge, but mentally, it was one of the hardest things I ever had to endure. Returning to the dojo the next day with a painful broken nose, knowing that someone might punch me in the same spot was also a real test of mental courage. There was absolutely no chance of taking a day off unless you couldn't physically stand and even then, they would probably wheel you in to at least practice your blocks and punches!

My first wife said that she was attracted to me because I was always laughing and joking with other students in the dojo, but during the *kenshusei* course, I rarely even smiled and became a very different person, even in the safe and warm environment of my home. I was physically and mentally drained and this weighed heavily on my otherwise cheerful and positive character. When we made it to the final training session just before the start of the two week Christmas and New Year holiday, I stood in the shower enjoying the hot water nursing my aches and pains and with the biggest smile I'd ever experienced on my face. For I knew, that I would not have to attend the dojo for the next fourteen days. Fourteen days of freedom without fear. When I arrived home that night my wife must have thought she had the old Pemba back, laughing and smiling. The next day I woke up expecting to feel equally elated, but it had dawned on me that after today I would only have thirteen days before I had to return to the dojo. I went to bed that night not feeling anywhere as happy as I did the previous night. The next morning I felt damn right miserable, as all I could focus on was the fact that I only had twelve more days before I had to return to the dojo. My growing anxiety and misery continued to increase every day of that holiday until all I wanted was to get back to the dojo to put myself out of the misery of waiting.

Two years later it seemed my feelings towards the *kenshusei* course hadn't lightened. I had just won the Kuwait International Championship and a journalist quipped, 'You must be the happiest man here today,' to which I responded, 'of course I'm happy that I won, but now I have to return to Japan and continue with the *kenshusei* course.' I'm not sure he understood the point I was making. I hadn't expected to achieve 1st place in *kumite* in Kuwait and it bought a lot of attention, not only from the press, but also one of the Kuwait Princes who presented me with a beautiful silk navy blue suit, which I continue to treasure even today. He even upgraded my seat to first class on the flight home, where in the company of Yahara sensei I felt like a complete fish out of water with the first class service provided to me. In fact I remember being envious of the people in economy class, as they lounged and ate carefree, where I sat there feeling very self-conscious of my faded jeans and roll neck attire and the unpronounceable options on the menu. Even with the memories of Kuwait still fresh and the distractions of the flight, I just sat there in my oversized seat feeling miserable with the prospect of returning to the dojo to continue the *kenshusei* course.

The human mind operates with unusual logic sometimes, that we can fear the waiting more than the event. I remember seeing a good friend get in a complete panic about going to a dentist appointment that wasn't due for a few days, and later, when I asked him how it went he dismissed it as though it was nothing. The fear of waiting had far outweighed the experience itself.

Wednesday was supposed to be a more relaxed day in the dojo where we would prepare food for the sensei and have time for self-training. But the 'self' part of the training was often interrupted by a sensei wishing to polish his *kumite* skills or even directing you to train on one of your weak areas. Yahara-sensei seemed particularly keen to develop my *makiwara* skills (punching a pad attached to a plank of wood), and would command me to hit the *makiwara* three hundred left and then three hundred right. He did not wait around to see if I followed his command to the full, but he would always return later and inspect my knuckles. Such was his level of expertise, he could tell just by the ripped flesh on my knuckles as to whether I had followed his instructions fully.

It was quite normal to be in the dojo from 10am until 3pm, which meant being in a constant state of alertness and fear. We also returned in the evenings and on Saturdays to assist the senior sensei in the regular classes. So while on paper the course looked manageable, in reality it was a huge physical and mental challenge; a challenge that would last for three years. When I finally made it to the shower room, a small cubical that transported me away from the fear and worry of the dojo, I stood there under the hot shower, away from everyone, away from that fearful command, "TAMANG, let's go," I would stand there for what seemed ages letting the hot water nurse over my body, and thanking God for being alive.

Even though the training was brutal, the lessons allowed us to go deep into our study of karate, to truly understand the technical beauty of this Japanese art. I had the great honour of learning from the likes of Ueki, Tanaka, Abe, Asai and of course, Nakayama-sensei. I felt a huge sense of pride after my first year examination when Nakayama-sensei informed me that my karate had improved a lot, he even offered me the position of *sen-nin*, which meant I would receive a small salary for teaching in the dojo. While it was a great privilege, the *sen-nin* salary was too small to even cover my rent, let alone food, so after three months I approached Abe- sensei and requested to return to *ken-nin,* status which didn't pay a salary but allowed me more time to take part-time work and support myself. I also had the great honour of walking Nakayama-sensei home after our first year graduation ceremony, where we also welcomed the new recruits. It saddens me to think that I was the last person to see him in good health, as the next day he slipped into a state of illness that would take his life.

As time went on, I adjusted both mentally and physically to cope with the course. It was interesting seeing the new recruits enter their first year as *kenshusei* as we graduated to the second. Watching them in the 'head lights' of coping under extreme pressure of attack made me realise how far we had come in a year. However, my fear and anxiety didn't change much in my second year, and if anything, it was made worse by having to wait more, as the first year *kenshusei* now had the privilege of fighting the sensei first, while we kneeled and waited in anticipation at the horrors that awaited us. It seemed waiting and worrying was something with which I struggled to come to grips.

As we neared the end of the course, I thought nothing about what I would do next. I only had enough energy to concentrate on the here and now, and even though my wife was anxious to talk about the future, all I could think about was surviving the *kenshusei* course. Reaching the end so I could resume a happy and cheerful life and then finally, that day arrived!

(Pads used to cover the makiwara (striking board) in the dojo)

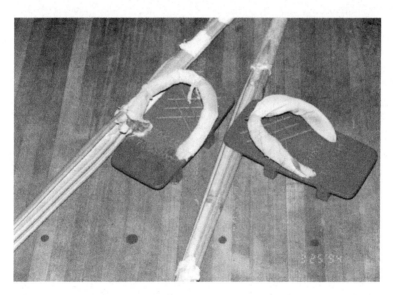

(Iron sandals and shinai (stick) used in training)

(First year *Kenshusei* graduation ceremony attended by Nakayama Sensei, myself, Yoko and three new recruits, April 1987)

(Final graduation ceremony in 1989, with myself, Naka, Nakamura and Aramoto)

(Yahara-sensei and *embu* performance in Kuwait 1988)

(Meeting the Kuwait Prince at the 1988 tournament)

Chapter 7 The Break Up

It was to be the biggest day of my life, but like many occasions when so much is happening, it went by in a blur. We had assembled in the dojo, all the instructors and senior students, all there to congratulate us on graduating the *kenshusei* course. Myself, Yoko Nakamura, Nobuyuki Aramoto and Tatsuya Naka all graduating, the last two, having entered from university so needing only two years to complete the course, but for Yoko and I it was three years of blood, sweat and tears. I gasped to think just how much blood I'd spilt on the dojo floor in the past three years; maybe enough for a healthy donation to a blood bank. I must have sweat my entire body weight a hundred times over, and as for the tears, they rained down so hard, but always inside of me.

It was not only a ceremony for our graduation but also a ceremony to welcome the new recruits to the *kenshusei* course. How little they knew about what was ahead of them. I resisted the urge to spoil the party and greeted them with the usual cry of *gambatte* (good luck). After the ceremony and dojo party, we continued the celebrations into the night and slowly, the euphoric feeling of relief began to wash over me. It was a good feeling, in fact, a great feeling! To have endured and survived such deep and meaningful training, though the meaningful understanding of my training would filter through later, over the next twenty years, guiding not just my karate but also my life.

The celebrations that day distracted me from fully reflecting on what graduating meant to me, but as I think about it now, it was the greatest moment in my life, in terms of personal accomplishments. I recall with great happiness, when I first gained my *shodan* and became *kumite* champion in Kuwait, but nothing that went before, or would come after, gave me such a great sense of accomplishment. Graduating the kenshusei was a different kind of happiness, I guess it's the sheer scale of the relief, combined with the happiness of graduating a course that at that time, less than seventy people in the world had achieved. I was now a JKA qualified professional instructor and one of only two foreigners to achieve this under the old, original JKA regime.

The other graduate was Malcolm Fischer who for many years was a big character in the dojo. However, during my second year on the course a disagreement flared up between Yahara-sensei, another huge character and Fischer, which led to Malcolm being expelled from the JKA and more worryingly for me, the JKA having a meeting to discuss whether non-Japanese had the right characteristics to participate in the *kenshusei* course. It was even asked if I should be allowed to continue, being the only foreigner currently on the course. I later discovered that all the instructors on the committee voted a unanimous 'yes' that I should be allowed to continue the course. I think my cause was helped by the fact that I had started at the dojo with just a white belt and spent almost seven years training hard and showing my respect for karate and the sensei that taught there. I believe I was the first graduate of the *kenshusei* course to start at the *hombu dojo* as a white belt. Naturally, I was proud of what I'd achieved at the JKA and very grateful to the instructors committee for allowing me to graduate. It would be another ten years before another foreigner was permitted to enter the course under the new JKA.

After the celebrations were over, I felt exhausted, completely burnt out. It was this feeling of 'burn out' that made me think I needed a fresh start, so my first wife and I went to live in Nepal. I had no plan to become a senior instructor at the JKA and had no real plans about what I should do with my life in Japan. For the past three years I hadn't considered anything other than the *kenshusei*. Once the course had finished there was this immediate feeling of emptiness, what was the purpose of my life now? It seemed natural to run away from Japan and go back to my roots and see my family.

For about eight months, my wife and I drifted between Nepal and India teaching karate wherever I could, opening new dojos and organising camps and tournaments. I wouldn't say I felt settled during this period but it was necessary for me to be around my own country for a while and I'm sure with the passage of time, I would become more settled, build a house, teach karate full time and allow the memories of the *kenshusei* course to become distant. Though they say, life happens between plans!

I can't say exactly how long it lasted but for many months afterwards I would wake in the night looking for the clock to see how long I had before I needed to go to the dojo. I remember suffering these feelings vividly when I was on the *kenshusei* course. Waking in the early hours, looking over at the clock, sometimes hearing the birds chirping outside and then feeling very anxious, knowing I had just a couple more hours before I had to be at the dojo and the punishment would start. For some strange reason, this habit continued for about seven months afterwards in India and Nepal, except there was no *hombu dojo* to attend, no highly skilled sensei to fight; just my own dojo, where I was the sensei and no fear or anxiety could exist. Sometimes I would find myself bolt upright staring hard at the surroundings of my dark room, trying to remind myself that I was in Nepal and not Tokyo. I guess you could liken it to some kind of post-traumatic stress, though thankfully, I didn't have flashbacks of Kagawa-sensei's powerful *mawashi geri* roundhouse hitting my face, or Yahara-sensei's fearsome spinning *uraken uchi* (back fist strike). I was most definitely grateful for being away from all that.

Then one day, news came that the JKA had split. Yahara-sensei called me personally while I was teaching in India. Hearing about the split stirred some deep emotions within me, almost like my family, I had grown to love, was in trouble and splitting in all directions. I felt obligated to return to Japan. I knew I had no control over the split, but I felt I had to be there, which unfortunately meant taking sides.

I returned to one of the most bizarre sights you could ever imagine seeing in a dojo of this calibre and reputation. Two distinct groups training side by side, going through their training; practicing *kihon*, *kata* and *kumite*, yet instruction coming from two different sources. Asai-sensei's group on one side and Nakahara-sensei's group on the other side and ironically four security guards placed between the two groups to prevent any breaches of security. I say ironically, as I wondered how these four security guards would handle the situation if tensions flared and all-out war broke. Four men standing between a fearsome array of karate talent. In the red corner weighing in with over 200 years of karate experience between them, Asai, Abe, Yahara, Kagawa, and Isaka-sensei, and in the blue corner weighing in with an equal amount of experience, Osaka, Tanaka, Ueki and Shoji-sensei. It would have been quite a spectacle had a fight broke out, but I'm pleased to say it never happened. Thankfully the Japanese have a higher regard for rules and procedure and the very presence of the security guards ensured those rules were never broken. It would have been extremely sad to see brothers fighting each other for real, and not in the spirit of *karate-do*. The only fighting that went on was in the court rooms as the two groups fought over who would retain the name JKA.

My first training session in the Ebisu dojo under the split regime was extremely awkward. I felt allegiances to all of them. In a sense, all of them had been like a father, in karate terms, all teaching me something, all winning my respect and admiration and all dishing out rough love in the form of a kick to the head or punch to the stomach! They were my family and now I was being asked to choose between them.

Tanaka-sensei had been the first sensei I'd met when I first entered the dojo and gave me first lesson in reality over gaining my *shodan* in two months and he had also approved my application to take my *shodan*, even though I didn't meet the two year requirement. Abe-sensei, along with the other members of the instructors committee, many made up from Nakahara-sensei's group had allowed me to remain on the *kenshusei* course after the Malcolm Fischer debacle. It was a terribly difficult decision but I had to go with my gut feeling and side with Asai-sensei's group, which included Yahara-sensei.

I felt a certain obligation to Yahara-sensei that would continue for many years. I was of course in awe of his skill. He had presented my application, though cautiously to Asai-sensei to join the *kenshusei* course and Asai-sensei had also approved this and passed it on to Nakayama-sensei. He had also taken a special interest in my training and coached me on many things and it was Yahara-sensei that had made the effort to contact me in India and inform me of the situation at the JKA. It was also one of those occasions where you couldn't be seen wavering on which group to choose, if you attempted to position yourself in the middle you would run the risk of losing face with both groups, so a decision had to be almost immediate. I half- heartedly sided with Asai-sensei's group. I say half-heartedly because I was completely against the split and hoped they could resolve their differences, but unfortunately that wasn't going to happen and any form of hesitation from me would have been viewed as weak spirited.

As the new decade began (1990) things weren't any easier outside the dojo as my wife and I were occupying floor space in her sister's apartment. I had also began working on a building site in the daytime which left me very little time and energy for the dojo. Unfortunately, it was a pivotal time in the dojo, with both groups looking to prove they were the strongest and had the greater right to the JKA name. Efforts had been made by both groups to recruit as many students as possible to their cause. It was also important to show the superiority of one group over the other. The Dubai championship was approaching and Yahara-sensei insisted I compete to help underline our group's strength and what better way than to show competitive edge at this upcoming world tournament. For me, it couldn't have come at a worse time in terms of my work and living situation. Training for a world tournament requires at least 3-4 hours of training per day, so it wasn't an ideal time because of my work commitment to prepare for such a big tournament but it was important to compete and defend the honour of Asai sensei's group at the Dubai JKA World Championship.

It was a big challenge to work full time and prepare for such a big tournament, during the day when I should have been preparing my *kata* and *kumite*, I was knee deep in sand and cement. This is when I discovered a new dojo, one without a tense and potentially explosive atmosphere. This dojo was set in the grounds of Myohoji Temple, just a short walk from our apartment. A beautiful setting on a dusty floor with no dividing line or security guards, just open space, open air and a beautiful silvery moon watching over. It was a beautiful place to train and it made me think about when Funakoshi- sensei would train under the watchful eye of Master Azato, his lantern and the glowing moon. For me it was a beautiful time, away from the politics and tension of the Ebisu dojo, a chance to go deep into my *kata* and *kumite* techniques. It was of course exhausting, working eight physical hours a day, knocking things down, clearing rubble, fetching cement and other building materials, then returning home briefly for dinner and then to the temple grounds to practice for a couple of hours. Somehow, even with all the pressure and exhaustion of trying to earn a living and train for a major world tournament I still managed to achieve 3rd place in the *kumite* at the Dubai tournament.

As an instructor in Asai-sensei's group, I had a following of students that would regularly attend my classes and not only was it my responsibility to teach them, but as Japanese custom would have it, when out socialising I was expected to pick up the majority of the bill. This of course benefited me during my *kushikai* days when the hierarchy system worked in my favour and the yakuza boss picked up the bill, but financially I was in no position to shoulder this responsibility, especially as my wife and I had used what little money we had to finally move from her sister's floor to our own apartment. Not wishing to shirk my responsibility completely, I began inviting my students over to my apartment where I would prepare some traditional Indian and Nepalese dishes along with beer purchased from the supermarket, at least now I could have some control over the bill. It seemed to be 'a hit' with my students and they began to comment on how nice the food tasted, they even suggested I open my own Nepalese restaurant.

Encouragement from my students to open a restaurant coincided with an empty space that had started to develop in my life. It had been two years since my last major tournament in Dubai and I had begun to commit myself less and less to tournaments, finally deciding to bring an end to my competition days. I had competed a lot over the years and reached my peak at the Kuwait Championships in 1988, so I felt now was the right time to retire. Retiring from competitions would leave a huge void in my life and of course I would miss the adrenaline that came with preparing and competing at a major tournament, so I felt it necessary to my character to fill the void with a new challenge. So in 1993 began my career in the restaurant business, and my wife and I opened our first restaurant in the vibrant part of Komagome.

Starting the restaurant also proved to be a good distraction from the politics and tension at the dojo, but on our opening night, I was full of nerves and doubt. For the past two years I had entertained many students with my food and light atmosphere, sometimes even breaking out the guitar, but the prospect of doing it professionally worried me. I had no professional training and my only experience in a restaurant was washing dishes. The food I made was adapted from what I learned from my mother or were simply experiments. So many questions raced through my mind: What if no one comes? What if they come and they don't like the food? What if they come, like the food, but I don't have enough to serve them? The questions and doubts were driving me crazy. Thankfully the restaurant grew in popularity and we began to receive regular customers and an income that could support my wife and I.

The power struggle between the two groups was also heating up. Nakahara's group conceded the Ebisu dojo, which on reflection was a clever move since the rent in Ebisu was one of the highest in the city and with only half the students now attending, it was impossible to cover the cost. It felt very empty when Nakahara-sensei's group finally left the dojo, leaving the security guards jobless. Eventually we also conceded the Ebisu dojo, the *hombu dojo* that Nakayama had worked so hard to build up during his life. It was the place where the JKA began and saw its most successful years, a wooden floor that had been witness to so many great *karateka* as they built their reputations and developed their skills. Sadly, it would become a knick knack and gift store. Not a fitting end for such an illustrious dojo, but like many things in life, out with the old and in with the new.

(Photo-shoot with the legendary Asai sensei)

(Teaching at the JKA Hombu dojo in Ebisu)

Chapter 8 Flying High

Like with all things new, it takes a little time to adjust. We moved to a smaller dojo in Shirogane in 1994, and without the presence of the Nakahara group, we were left with a noticeably smaller group of students. We were still the JKA, but the dojo desperately needed to be worn in. It was a new start and with the other group gone, in theory, the atmosphere could return to that of a normal hard- working dojo, instead of the conflict and resentment that was noticeably in the air at the Ebisu dojo. I felt a little less pressure, and was able to enjoy teaching there on a Saturday, leaving the majority of my time to concentrate on my new restaurant. This began to pay off as the restaurant became more and more popular with a legion of regulars, and a constant stream of new customers. For the first time in my life I began to feel financial comfort, and felt I'd come a long way from the days of surviving on thirty five yen noodles and free samples from the food courts of Ikebukoro.

I was a senior instructor in one half of the JKA and was now the owner, along with my wife, of a successful Nepalese restaurant in a vibrant part of the city. I had a comfortable apartment and a nice group of friends, both within karate and outside of karate. I even began performing songs late at night in my restaurant, and enjoyed the praise received from my singing and guitar skills. Life was good.

With tournaments no longer a focus I could enjoy teaching and of course, continue to learn from the likes of Asai, Abe, Kagawa and Yahara-sensei. Pressure is sometimes a good catalyst for training, but it's also nice to have a period where you can let your mind roam freely, unhindered by pressure, and use the time to examine and ponder some of the deeper questions relating to karate. This was not always possible during the *kenshusei* course or the constant strained atmosphere of the final year in the Ebisu dojo. I could feel my karate growing in a different way and I began to see how the lessons related to other areas of my life. For example, in running a busy restaurant there always seemed a quicker and more efficient way to do things. I was constantly making little adjustments to my kitchen to make my cooking and preparation of food technically easier and this was the same with my guitar playing. I had taught myself from a young age, so I had no classical training in reading music or understanding chords, but it seemed the tiny adjustments I made when playing, improved the sound incrementally over time. This is the essence of good karate, to identify and adjust until perfection is reached. If this is applied to everything else, then so much can be achieved in all areas of our life. But maintaining this philosophy is not as easy as it sounds when you consider the wealth of distractions and complications that exist in our lives.

I could also see noticeable improvements in my life by making the decision to quit drinking alcohol. Like many people do I had fallen into the trap of associating socialising with friends with drinking alcohol, this had started during my *kushikai* group days and continued for a long time, though with noticeably less volume during the *kenshusei* course. I had begun to see alcohol as a way to relax during more stressful times, though unfortunately whilst it seemed to take the edge off things while I was drinking, it magnified everything else when sobering up. It was becoming a risk to both my physical and mental health.

After six months of being teetotal I really began to see the clarity in my mind and my energy for things really picked up. This led me to begin knew things like writing songs and painting. I'd played the guitar for many years now but never felt inspired to write any songs but a new wave of enthusiasm had taken hold and I felt I need to express myself more fully with song and painting. I was also starting to experience the fruits of my earlier labour, with my dojos in India, Nepal and Sri Lanka going from strength to strength. In fact the Nepalese dojo had attracted a lot of interest from the Nepalese Royal family, especially from the Crown Prince who had attended the initial opening ceremony. My family were originally from Nepal before moving to Darjeeling, so after my success in Kuwait in 1988, I had become a bit of a hero in that country, regularly reported by the press and receiving a lot of attention whenever I visited. At that time Nepal didn't really have any celebrated athletes so hearing that a poor boy, originally from Nepal had achieved so much in karate had given the locals something to be proud of, and for me, a kind of celebrity status with regular invitations to the Nepalese Palace. On one trip to Nepal I remember over 100 students all lined up in the arrival terminal, waiting to present me with a traditional necklace of flowers called *mala*. I had experienced adoration from afar when I'd witnessed students' show their respect to famous sensei's like, Nakayama, Tanaka and Asai-sensei but my own direct experience of this in Nepal gave me very mixed feelings. In all honesty, it made part of me a little arrogant but then I would be reminded by my own roots and be humbled by the experience. Being a guest at the

Nepal Palace added to my momentary feelings of grandeur and of course, it was a great honour to me and something I continue to be proud of, especially as it was during very happy times and before the terrible tragedy that would befall the Nepalese Royal family.

I was also part of Yahara sensei's entourage so would often travel to many countries to assist him with his seminars and teaching. This was a great opportunity to meet many European *karateka* and to further build my reputation from my competition days. It was also a great to visit some of the famous sites in countries like, Greece and France and all while following my passion for karate. I indeed felt very lucky and grateful to the position my life had bought me. However, I reminded myself, that it was no fluke that I was in this position. I had arrived in Japan over eighteen years ago with the sole intention of studying 'real' karate and obtaining my black belt in two months. Whilst I did not initially achieve this and later returned to Japan to complete this goal, I was always completely focused on achieving my black belt. After that, I was focused on becoming the strongest fighter in the *kushikai* group, and then to complete the *kenshusei* course. I always had a clear focus and direction on what I wanted to achieve, sometimes my next goal came about accidently, like starting my first restaurant, but once committed my focus never wavered.

Focus and hard work rewarded me with my current situation, riding high on being a senior international instructor for one half of the JKA, a thriving restaurant which now employed staff, Royal friends and celebrity status in Nepal. It was very easy to be caught up in the moment and lose track of what is truly important, and before I knew it cracks began to appear in all aspects of my life.

My growing success as an international instructor meant that I began to spend more and more time away from Japan and my wife. I left her to run our restaurant for long periods of time and generally became detached from our home life which inevitably put a strain on our marriage. Even when I was home I did little to repair those cracks, and in all honesty and regrettably I had become a little arrogant due to my higher status both in Japan and abroad. Eventually we reached the end of the road and we divorced in 1998. For the majority I felt responsible for the marriage failure and I also felt a deep appreciation towards my ex-wife, as without her it's unlikely that I would have joined or completed the *kenshusei* course. This fuelled my decision to give both the apartment and the restaurant to my now ex-wife.

(The Crown Prince of Nepal attending the opening ceremony
At my Kathmandu dojo, Nepal in 1994 with Abe sensei (left))

Chapter 9 Fallen

Sometimes life moves gently up and down as we experience the higher and lower points of our existence, and I had just experienced an extreme high point in my life with my successful karate and restaurant career, but what seemed like a blink of an eye, this was all about to change.

After giving up my apartment and restaurant to my ex-wife I had two choices, to once again stay on friends floors until I had the money for my own apartment or sleep in the one thing I had left, my beaten up old car. I opted for the car as felt broken inside after my thirteen year marriage coming to an end and I didn't want to show my friends the pain I was experiencing. I've always been a sensitive sleeper, even a change in pillow can prevent me from getting a good night sleep, yet I found it very easy to sleep in my car, parked close to the park so I could make use of the toilet facilities. I did this for three months, only occasionally accepting the hospitality of a friend's floor or sofa. It's surprised me how, when necessary, the mind and body can adapt to any situation.

Spending so much time alone in my car and around the park gave me far too much time for some unhealthy reflection on my life. I was close to reaching forty years old and this also weighed extremely heavily on my sense of where I was today and what I had lost. I was also thinking a lot about home and some of the things I had missed over the years, like spending time with my eldest brother before he passed away. I had of course returned home for the funeral, but seeing my family, especially my elderly mother fending for herself weighed heavily on my heart, almost, like I had been letting them down by being away from them all this time. I felt my mind was stretched across so many problems, with my concerns for my family in Darjeeling, in Japan with karate and the end of my marriage. I felt a lot of confusion and distress in my life and in many ways I was lost, completely unsure of where life was leading me and how to apply 'the brakes' to move again in the right direction.

I can honestly say that I have never felt so beaten up inside and was hugely tempted to give up my life in Japan and return to Nepal where I was still a hero and a friend to the Crown Prince, but my pride would not let me give up on a life that had took twenty years to build. My character was also incapable of walking away from a challenge, or as it felt at the time, a fight. A fight to save my life in Japan and return it to a happy mental state, the idea of just throwing the towel in and returning home would have probably weighed even more heavily on my mind and done even more damage in the long run.

So, if escaping wasn't an option and I felt I had to stay and face the pain, part of me was tempted to at least numb the pain and start drinking again. I remembered how alcohol used to make me feel, it could really take the edge off things and sometimes lead me to answers. However, I knew my character well and knowing that I don't do things by half. I think had I chosen this escape from misery there would have been no coming back for me, I would either be one of those poor unfortunate souls you see on the streets begging for money for their next fix, or more likely, dead! It sounds dramatic but I know my character, so luckily for me I opted for a better route.

Twenty years of training at the JKA dojo, competing at world tournaments and completing the *kenshusei* course, had taken my physical abilities to a level that I never thought possible and this isn't meant to sound boastful, it's a simple 'numbers' thing; my kenshusei years alone amounted to training five days a week, around 4-5 hours of training a day for three years, anyone would have experienced a similar increase in ability and this applies to any discipline. But at this moment it wasn't the physical improvements I was grateful for, but the mental strength and spirit I had gained during that time, in all honesty, the experience I gained training at the JKA may well have saved my life.

I remember being on my knees; battered, bruised and exhausted after fighting Kagawa-sensei and then looking up the line and seeing that I still had to fight Yahara and Tanaka-sensei, with a feeling of absolute hopelessness sweeping over me, yet somehow I made it through that, not just once but week in week out for three years. A failed marriage and living in my car I was 'on my knees' but I was reminded that it wasn't anything I couldn't handle. It seemed hopeless but if I just picked myself up, trusted my abilities, kept things simple and remained persistent in my cause I could find happiness again.

I kept things simple by taking jobs that didn't require too much pressure, opting for a delivery job that meant driving late at night to deliver bottles of drinks to over 50 convenience stores on the west side of Tokyo, this often involved driving over 400km a night but I found this existence for a while quite peaceful. Tokyo is a far less hectic place in the early hours of the morning. It was a long hot summer in 1998 so swapping the high humidity of the daytime for the coolness of the night wasn't such a bad choice. It also gave me the solitude I craved for at the time. Engaging in long conversations with people, including good friends had become very difficult for me, I just wanted to be left alone with my thoughts.

This feeling also spurred me to approach Asai-sensei and ask him for a sabbatical from my teaching and training duties, and he was very gracious in understanding my situation. For the next six months I would concentrate on rebuilding my life and repairing my heart, karate training for me would continue but alone late at night in the park.

After a few months, driving over 400km a night and sleeping in my car was starting to take its toll and I began to think about what was next for me. By coincidence I received a call from a good friend who was a real estate agent and he informed me that he had found a new place to start a restaurant. I told him that I hadn't been looking for a new restaurant and could never afford the rent in Tokyo, but he reassured me that this place was very cheap and I should at least come and have a look. Naturally I felt a little intrigued.

We met outside a building in a not-so-vibrant area of Tokyo, called Otsuka where he led me down the steps to a rundown basement bar which had previously been a snack bar. The Japanese snack bar isn't to be confused with a brothel, though some of the names given to these late night drinking holes often raise suspicion, but for most snack bars they are the stop between work and home for many salary men where light snacks are served along with beer, whiskey and good conversation. The interior was extremely drab with the heavy lingering smell of cigarette smoke, it was also full of the previous tenants junk. From a restaurant perspective it was completely unhygienic and therefore unusable, however, if I agreed to rent it at half the price I was free to refurbish and turn it into a restaurant. I was desperate to get back on my feet again and out of my car, but with no money, the refurbishment would take months and months of hard work. I looked again at the bar and saw all the clutter and mess and it kind of reminded me of the inside of my mind. It would take a lot of physically hard work and sacrifice to turn this mess into a comfortable, clean fully functioning restaurant that could become a happy environment for me and the people that visited. I felt a connection between the bar and my state of mind and felt by clearing one will help the other. I told my friend I would take the bar!

As soon as I got the keys to my new restaurant, I began work on it right away. Thirty six hours later I suddenly realized I had barely stopped, only occasionally to eat a light snack and drift off in to a light snooze with my back and head against the filthy wall. It was hard work and I could have made life a lot easier for me by calling on the help of friends and even my students, they would have been happy to lend a hand and I would have got the restaurant ready in half the time, but I felt really strongly that this was something I had to do completely alone, every bit of junk I removed, wall I stripped, area I cleaned was all part of the process of rebuilding myself. It also felt like a form of penance, to make a mends for my previous mistakes in my life.

After an intense two months of refurbishing it was now beginning to look like a restaurant, apart from one major detail, a lack of tables and chairs and other furniture commonly found in a restaurant. I began scouring Tokyo for old tables and chairs and was lucky to find a restaurant in the process of refurbishment that was happy to dump their old stuff on me. Finally I was ready to open to customers, but I had used all my savings setting the restaurant up, though luckily I managed to borrow a small amount of money from a friend to buy enough things to offer a reasonable menu, and soon opening night was upon me. Once again, I felt that pang of doubt; whether anyone would come, would I be able to pay my friend back, will I earn enough money to cover the next rent, electricity and gas bills. So many questions worried me that night and continued to worry me, and I wondered if this was how life would always be, full of self-doubt and financial concern.

Due to the less vibrant location and the decline in fortunes of the Japanese economy, the popularity of my new restaurant developed painfully slow, and I often found myself sitting there late at night waiting for customers to come. After a few months it began to pick up and covering the rent became less of a concern. However, there still wasn't enough income for me to be able to afford rent on an apartment, so I slept in the restaurant for the first few months and reacquainted myself with the local *sento* (bathhouse). Being a basement restaurant, there was very little natural light so this did not help my overall mental state.

Slowly, the signs of success with my new restaurant venture became noticeable, as a handful of customers began to return on a regular basis—and like many times throughout my restaurant career—these customers became very good friends. One customer in particular used to catch my eye. She was called Mari, and she seemed so free and gentle, a delicate beauty that had travelled the world, she lit up the restaurant when she laughed and smiled. I felt very drawn to her, but I was still in the aftermath of a divorce and really just trying to keep a grip on the small things I'd been working hard to get. Nevertheless, our friendship began to blossom.

Things were improving financially as my restaurant started to build up some regular customers. I had been using the restaurant to sleep in and also when I didn't have time to go to the park, or it was raining, I was using it as my own personal dojo, as no matter how tired I was or short of time it was essential to my state of mind and body to do some kind of karate training every day. I guess there was one benefit of my restaurant being at basement level, as it was completely private during the daytime so ideal for training in. However, working and living between the same walls every day was starting to make me a little stir crazy, then coincidently I got a phone call from my estate agent friend. He insisted on showing me this apartment in the quiet part of Komagome, and I was struck by the amount of greenery that surrounded the apartment, which was quite unusual for such a central Tokyo location. I was also in awe of the *Sakura* (cherry blossom) tree that was in direct view from the balcony. The apartment felt perfect, though the only problem was the rent was twice as much as anything I'd experienced in the past. Fortunately one of my students visiting from Mexico was also looking for a place to stay so I was able to share the apartment with him.

After closing the restaurant every night I would choose to walk back to the apartment in Komagome from Otsuka, and whilst it was 30 minutes' walk it took me through a part of Tokyo that was less well lit, meaning there were less neon signs and high rise buildings that stayed illuminated all night. Finally I had the chance to see stars in the sky, something I hadn't seen much of in the twenty years I'd lived in Tokyo. This gave me great energy and comfort and I further embraced this by finding an emergency ladder on the side of my apartment building that took me to the top of the roof. The nearest major building to our apartment block was a primary school, and at night it was completely blacked out which meant there was no interfering light as I gazed up at the stars.

I started to become excited towards the end of my shift at the restaurant, to return home and climb the ladder, coffee in hand and just lie back on the surface of the roof and gaze up at the sky. It became a very euphoric and spiritual experience for me and I would often drift off into a light sleep. On one occasion, and this will probably sound quite unbelievable to most people reading this, but I was meditating very deeply on the roof under the beautiful night sky, when I felt my spirit lift into the sky and become surrounded by stars, it was the most surreal experience of my life so far, and even though I tried on many occasions to repeat this experience, it only ever happened once and it inspired me to write my first song, '*Sorano hoshi – Arigato*' which means the star in the sky, thank you! I had chosen so much solitude over the past few months that the stars felt like my only constant company and I felt extremely grateful for this wonder.

Life was becoming more bearable, I was slowly lifting from my knees!

(Mari and I at my restaurant in Otsuka)

Chapter 10 Getting Up

I realise now that I spent over a year and a half in a state of forced solitude, barely communicating with people unless I really had to, not watching TV or even socialising with friends, instead just a very simple life of work, training, painting and playing the guitar. With my mind no longer clouded with so much tension and with the good company of the stars at night, I began to imagine what it would be like to spend time with the nice lady that often came to my restaurant. I finally plucked up the courage to ask her out and was very happy when she accepted.

She also had a lot of passion for nature and walking in the mountains, so we would often take the train to some of the surrounding mountain ranges. Visiting the mountains with Mari reminded me how important nature is to my mental well-being. I had forgotten this during the past few years, which probably, unnecessarily added to my tension. Escaping the hustle and bustle of Tokyo for a day, walking with and talking to Mari in the mountains was just the tonic I needed after a tough few years of struggling. We talked constantly, sharing our life experiences and I began to see her as a kindred spirit. Sharing some of my woes from the past really helped me come to terms with them, and most importantly, put them to rest. We learnt much about each other and instead of the worries and complication that sometimes comes when starting a new relationship, everything seemed simple and natural and fell into place as so it should.

As well as my new found company with the stars and the lovely Mari, I also felt energy from the *Sakura* tree that stood in front of my balcony and it reminded me of my childhood and the pine tree I had claimed when I was back in Darjeeling. At that point in my life I began to understand myself, my connection with nature and the things my mind needed to remain healthy and positive, it felt like a huge relief to finally 'get' myself, almost a spiritual enlightenment, and now that I understood myself better I could manage myself and steer towards happiness instead of the pain I had done so often in the past. This was quite an easy thing to do because happiness was now easy to find, all I had to do was spend more and more time with Mari. Eventually my student from Mexico decided to return home and it had been almost a year since Mari and I been together so it felt natural for her to move in and share the *Sakura* tree and stars with me!

I continued to train alone each day in the restaurant before customers arrived and was enjoying the freedom of not being embroiled in the politics of a large karate organisation. However, students would often visit my restaurant and bring me up to speed of the latest goings on. It seemed that cracks had begun to appear in our half of the JKA, with a clash of personalities developing between some of the senior sensei's.

This also coincided with the end of the ten year court battle over which group would retain the JKA name. The Nakahara group had succeeded in retaining the rights to this name which meant Asai-sensei's group was now in need of a new name, and as Asai-sensei saw it, a new direction, a direction that wouldn't include Yahara-sensei and any of his followers.

Asai-sensei formed the Japan Karate Shoto Federation (JKS), taking Kagawa-sensei and many of the students. Abe-sensei comprised the Japan Shotokan Karate Association (JSKA) and was happy to have a small organisation, since he felt that a big organisation led to one thing:

big problems! This left a small but skilful group of sensei's under Yahara-sensei, including Isaka, and Naito sensei.

At this point I wasn't really thinking about what would be my next move in karate, I was just happy to be fit and healthy and able to train alone in my restaurant. My restaurant, as I had hoped was becoming a place of happiness for me, a place to train, earn money to live, I was even starting to play the guitar and singing to some of my regular customers. Mari had also begun to help me out during the weekends and my sociable character was finally returning.

One evening Yahara-sensei visited my restaurant with news that he was starting his own organisation and would very much like me to join him. Whilst I wasn't thinking about getting involved in another dojo he caught me in a happy and optimistic frame of mind, I also still felt a great allegiance to Yahara-sensei as he had taught me so much during my career in karate and I respected his ability very highly, so I accepted his invitation. He had already built up quite a following, including the famous clothing designer, Yohji Yamamoto, who had offered us his own private dojo for our small group to begin training in. Yohji would later become a major sponsor of our next dojo and organisation. I was excited to become part of this new organisation but I also made a promise to myself, that in the event of things not working out, this would be the last time I involve myself in a major karate organisation.

My life was beginning to move forward on all fronts and what seemed like a blink of an eye, Mari and I were soon expecting our first child. When Yuta was born it brought a whole new and exciting dynamic to both our lives and as a new father it brought new responsibilities as I now had a new wife and a son to provide for. This gave me a new energy to get things right, to make sure that I never found myself in a situation of starting from the bottom again. In the past I had found myself in financial difficulty and sometimes relying on the hospitality of a friends floor or even sleeping in my car, but having a wife and son meant that I could never get myself into these difficulties again, having a regular income and a roof over our heads would take priority over everything, including karate. I began to work even harder to build my restaurant, ensuring new customers came as well as regular customers.

I kept my karate training up in the park and also attending Yohji Yamamoto private dojo to train with Yahara-sensei's group which had now formed the Karatenomichi World Federation (KWF) where Yahara-sensei had appointed me the director of the international division, hoping that my devoted students in India, Nepal and Sri Lanka would be a good place to start in building the organisation internationally. Yahara-sensei also had a big international following, so in reality, my role in international development was minor to his.

The newly formed KWF and its senior sensei's met often to discuss the direction of this new organisation and talked a lot about how not to repeat the mistakes of the past. As it was seen as important to portray the right image of power and success, we found a new dojo in a very expensive part of Tokyo called Shirokanedai in the autumn of 2001.

Yahara-sensei started to expand his organisation across the globe persuading many sensei from countries like South Africa, the UK, America and Greece, who were originally with the JKA, to join the KWF. I also brought my students from Nepal, India and Sri Lanka into the organisation so much was achieved in quite a short space of time.

After many years surrounded by conflict; the breakup of the JKA and my divorce, it seemed that life was in one of its quiet, less eventful cycles, which for me, was just fine. I did, however, have the occasional disagreement with Yahara-sensei, but overall, dojo life was more settled than the days of the JKA split. Though juggling running a restaurant, teaching in the dojo and now, the responsibilities of being a father, was proving very difficult. Something had to give, and for once, it would have been wrong of me to put karate first.

Karate for me had never been about making it a profession, in the sense that I would receive a salary to live. Having a restaurant served the purpose of providing an income and allowed me to never look at karate in the sense of financial gain. I made my request to Yahara-sensei to further reduce my teaching responsibilities which naturally led to arguments and questions about my overall commitment to the KWF. I countered by saying that my family comes first but was so committed to the KWF that I wouldn't take a salary for the remainder of my teaching commitments. I wanted to demonstrate my belief that for me, karate is just about training and sharing, that it's not a matter of politics or profit and who is deemed as giving more and being more worthy. Like my time at the JKA, both before and after the split and now my time in KWF, I just wanted to get on with training without all the unnecessary pressure and tension. I'd accepted that pressure and tension was part of the *kenshusei* course and a way to test a student's mettle, but now there was nothing left to prove. I guess, like most people, I just wanted an easy life and a chance to get on with the things that are important and not be hampered by things that are unnecessary for our well-being.

Mari and I had also begun visiting parks and local nature spots with our son Yuta and were very much enjoying this experience. We would often go to Shinjuku *gyoen* (park) and enjoy lunch sitting on the grass under some of the beautiful trees there. Like I had when I was a child, a great affection for the pine trees near my village, I was beginning to develop a great affection for the trees and nature that existed in the parks of Tokyo. There was even a very old and large tree in Shinjuku gyoen that I felt a special connection to and would meditate next to it whenever I had the opportunity, it really reminded me of my roots with nature, and when I left the tree to return to my apartment, amongst the crowds, cars and pollution I instantly longed to be back under the tree. This experience made me realise that it was time to go, once and for all.

We had also visited one of Mari's friends who lived in the mountains, a two hour drive from Tokyo in Yatsugatake and were amazed by the panoramic views of the snow-capped mountains. Visiting the mountains with Mari had brought me into contact with a whole different life that exists in Japan. I'd spent most of my Japanese life in Tokyo, and hadn't fully begun to appreciate the beauty of Japanese nature. Our weekend trips to the mountains made me realise that I could happily grow old in Japan, and still be amongst breath-taking scenery of mountains and forests. This is the environment I grew up in, and this is where I felt I needed to grow old. My wife and I had come to the conclusion that we had spent enough of our lives in one of the most densely populated cities in the world, and it was time to take our young son, Yuta, and be as close to nature as possible.

I was happy to see the KWF moving forward and expanding its membership throughout the world, but I was even happier that I was moving to the countryside to enjoy a more natural life. I had followed Yahara-sensei for over twenty years and learnt many things from him, we had our differences but I will always be respectful of what he taught me in karate, but my time with Yahara-sensei and the KWF was now over and a less hampered existence beckoned.

I had also enjoyed my love affair with Tokyo for twenty five years, which was the longest time I had stayed in one place. I had many great memories and experiences with this city but sometimes it's important to know when to say goodbye to things; I felt my decision to leave Tokyo came at exactly the right time in my life.

Chapter 11 Deep in Nature

My wife and I knew it wouldn't be easy. We had saved little for a deposit to buy a place, so it took a very understanding bank manager to help us secure the property we wanted in a beautiful mountain town just a couple of hours drive from Tokyo, called Kobuchizawa, located in the mountain region of Yatsugatake. The location of the property wasn't in a prime area of Kobuchizawa, but with other businesses surrounding it and being close to a main junction, we hoped we could attract enough customers to cover the mortgage payments and feed ourselves. It was another big life change, but this time, I had a warm feeling that it was going to be for the better and although we were starting again, like I had done many times before. Seeing the mountains every day gave me the energy and confidence that we would make a success of our new lives.

In May 2004 we said goodbye to all our customers and good friends by throwing one last parting in the Otsuka restaurant and was grateful to hear that many of them would come and visit us at our new restaurant, as Kobuchizawa is the perfect weekend getaway for those wanting to escape the crowds and stress of Tokyo. It was comforting to know that we would at least have the occasional weekend customers visiting from Tokyo.

Our new restaurant was nothing like the run-down snack shop I had to work with when I first moved to Otsuka. Despite that fact, the layout was just a regular family house, so once again I worked relentlessly to prepare the new restaurant for open day by converting the downstairs area into a twenty-seat restaurant with mountain views! It also helped that the local people were so welcoming and didn't seem threatened by the prospect of another restaurant competing for the limited and seasonal trade of the area. We were quick to make good friends and useful connections.

I had no real thoughts about what to do with my karate, only to continue training when and wherever I could. The surrounding mountains of Kobuchizawa provided me with the perfect dojo during those summer months. On breaks from the restaurant I would often jump in my car and drive to a secluded spot, walk for a while then practice karate, in a clearing in the forest, or even by a raging river or waterfall. Training here gave me renewed energy for everything, especially my family and new restaurant. Occasionally students would visit from Tokyo and we would use one of the local school halls to train in. Some of these students were from foreign countries like England and France, who had been training in Tokyo only, so the experience of walking in the mountains, training karate, relaxing in the *onsen* (hot baths) and enjoying a good meal at our new restaurant became the perfect tonic that would bring them back many times.

I hadn't long moved to Kobuchizawa when I received a phone call from a Sogabe *senpai* (senior) who led a group of karateka in Hokkaido, the northern Island of Japan. He had been a member of the JKA for many years and was looking to take his organisation in a more traditional direction. I was extremely flattered when he invited to become the chief instructor of his group called the Japan Shotokan karate-do Federation. I had made many visits to Hokkaido over the years and trained with Sogabe *senpai* (senior) many times and was a little taken back that he was inviting me to lead his group. I asked him for some time to think about his kind and flattering invitation.

As Mari and I became more and more involved in the local community people started to learn of my karate experience, especially with the JKA and they became intrigued about karate. It wasn't long before a number of locals were asking if I would teach them and their children. One local businessman, Mr Kikuhara, was so thrilled by the prospect of having an ex JKA instructor in town, that he donated half the building he was constructing for his offices as a dojo area. The location was perfect: just a few minutes' drive from my restaurant, and perched on a spot that gave panoramic views of Mt. Yatsugatake and the Southern Alps. Being constantly surrounded by these beautiful mountain ranges gave me a new lease of energy in all the areas of my life. It also reminded me that it was time to return home and visit my family in Nepal. I especially wanted to show my elderly mother her new grandson. As well as visiting family I also used the opportunity to hire a recording studio at a considerably cheaper rate than in Japan and using Mari's soft and gentle voice for backing vocals, we recorded twelve songs and called the album 'Deep in Nature,' as all the songs were inspired by nature. I wasn't planning or expecting to become an international recording artist, but after years of performing these songs in my restaurant, I decided it was time to record them for prosperity.

At this point of my life, I had no real plan in terms of my karate career; my only plan was to continue practicing every day and teaching a few local people and their children. I had devoted most of my life to karate so I felt it was time to devote myself to my family and a new life in

Kobuchizawa. Of course, I would always need to practice karate, but possibly not to the degree I had done so in the past. However, when you practice karate on a daily basis for most of your life and then you think you might reduce that practice to two or three times a week it doesn't work, at least not at my age. My body and mind required that I practice, even if just for half an hour, pretty much every day. It's not necessarily a bad thing to have this kind of reliance and I know many senior sensei's, including those over sixty and seventy years old who still practice with this frequency, possibly even more. The result is, they still have the strength and versatility of a man thirty years younger. I hope I can achieve this when I reach their age.

My mountain dojo was a relaxed place to train, and I wanted my new students to feel the energy from the mountains as they practiced diligently. Making the short drive to the dojo, taking in the breath-taking beauty of the mountains was a long way from fighting for space on the Yamanote Line to Meguro and then through the polluted streets to Shirokanedai. It was a very good place to teach, away from the political pressures that I had seen develop with all the organisations that I had been a part of during my twenty-five years in Tokyo. It was just me, a few diligent students and the mountains, but still Sogabe *senpai's* invitation to become chief instructor weighed heavily on my mind.

Sogabe *senpai* was a very nice and honest man. He admitted that he wasn't getting any younger and felt his organisation needed a younger and more experienced Chief Instructor to help develop it. I of course had my doubts about accepting the position, namely the idea of belonging to a large organisation again, since my experience had taught me that they always end up with egos clashing and political turmoil. I also felt a little out of my depth, to accept a Chief Instructor position in a large Japanese karate organisation was a huge honour, an honour that had been righty reserved for people like, Kagawa-sensei, after he became chief instructor at the JKS when Asai-sensei passed away, and Yahara-sensei at the KWF and of course Ueki-sensei at the JKA. These men are a generation above me, they were my sensei's, so the prospect of having a similar rank to them was very unsettling.

On the plus side, I saw this as a chance to show the world that people can come together and enjoy practicing karate without the unnecessary struggles that often resulted. I would also be a new Chief Instructor, not the perfect Chief Instructor, and as I had been schooled around so many great Chief Instructors like Nakayama-sensei, I had a clear vision of what made a great Chief Instructor and given time I could grow into this role.

Before I made my final decision to accept the Chief Instructors position, I flew to Hokkaido to meet with Sogabe *senpai* and other prominent members of this organisation in the winter of 2004. We trained a little, but most importantly we talked for many hours about what I wanted from a karate organisation and what they wanted from a Chief Instructor.

Essentially they wanted to follow the teachings originally laid down by Funakoshi-sensei and I responded that I could only teach Funakoshi-sensei's way through what was interpreted to me by Nakayama-sensei and other sensei's heavily involved with the development of the JKA. In fact, from a technical perspective, I could offer nothing more than I had learned at the JKA. I had not had the inclination during my years of training to alter what had been taught to me, as I felt the JKA was a perfect representation of shotokan karate. This pleased Sogabe *senpai* as he was concerned that karate was being watered down for competition purposes and was keen to follow a more traditional route.

I had some demands relating to the running of the organisation. First I wanted to change the name to Nihon Shotokan Karate-do Federation to reflect a more Japanese base. I wanted the *dojo kun* to be compulsory in all NSKF dojos, as this reflected Funakoshi-sensei's wishes. I agreed that they would continue to organise things in Japan whilst my main responsibilities were international development and technical direction. But my real stand was on the philosophy of the organisation. I was desperate not to repeat the mistakes of the past and passionate about an organisation that would allow serious karate students to develop not only their technical skill, but also, through the honest practice of karate, help them with their everyday lives and support their mental well-being as well. In essence, what Funakoshi-sensei had set out to do: build character as well as karate skill. It was a bold challenge, but I believed that if I was going to devote myself to a new organisation, it had to be on the terms that I would feel comfortable with. I was just being honest to myself, I knew both my limitations and my demands, I made it clear to Sogabe *senpai* what type of Chief Instructor he was trying to recruit. I'm happy to say, he graciously accepted me as the Chief Instructor of the Nihon Shotokan Karate-do Federation.

It pleases me greatly that the NSKF has grown steadily over the past few years, both locally in Japan and internationally, but I realise it takes many years to build something worthwhile, to develop good technical ability in students, and above all to get them to understand the purpose of karate and how it can have a profoundly positive effect on both their physical and mental well-being.

It's why I now write this book, to share my life story, my understanding and the practical application to studying karate. This is why this book is broken into three parts though hopefully all connecting. Part one details my life up until becoming the Chief Instructor of the NSKF, a life of many ups and downs and challenges that have shaped my understanding of life. Part 2 attempts to frame that understanding in a life philosophy that I hope readers will relate to. Part 3 is purely for students of karate, as I explain the application of what I've learnt in basic and advanced techniques.

(Opening ceremony at Kabuchizawa *hombu dojo*)

Chapter 12 My Way

There are many philosophies and religions that talk about being on a righteous path, journeying to a state of self-enlightenment as an ultimate goal. I felt that I stumbled on to the right path when I began karate. It wasn't a conscious choice, where I thought to myself, I need some clear direction in my life, but simply a desire to be physically strong and an outlet for my boisterous energy. I also always knew I had a close connection with nature thanks to growing up under the shadow of the Himalayas, so I always felt a desire to be as natural as possible. Karate didn't feel natural to me at first, but after many years of practice it feels like the most natural thing to do in my life—karate for me has been my guiding light through good times and bad. Many of us search for answers throughout our lives, and sometimes not in the right places, like at the end of a bottle. I'm glad to say, that after many years of searching sometimes in the wrong place, I found my answers through karate.

There is an important concept in shotokan karate that can be traced back to days of the samurai. *Ikken hissatsu*, the killing blow. The samurai were a highly-skilled class of warriors and trained incessantly to perfect their skills. When drawing their *katana* (a curved, slender single edged sword) in battle the goal was to kill their opponent with the minimal amount of moves, they even practised drawing their *katana* from their *koshirae* (sword scabbard) and with one swift and powerful cutting move kill or maim their opponent before sheathing the sword effortlessly. *Iaido*, the Japanese martial devoted to the *katana* still practises these moves, not believing that they have any practical use in today's world, but to understand the value of the practice and philosophy that goes with this ancient art. Like the samurai, they believed in power and efficiency in combat and when fighting multiples of attackers. This was a necessity for survival, thus the concept of *ikken hissatsu* was an important part of the samurai way.

In *karate-do* this concept remains, but not in the sense that the ultimate goal in karate is to train ourselves to kill or maim someone, but instead to pursue perfection in our technique to such a degree that one punch, kick or strike is all that is needed. This concept separates shotokan from other styles of karate and martial arts, where stamina and multiple techniques are considered more important. Of course, in shotokan, multiple techniques are practiced and stamina is developed to prepare for every eventuality in combat, but still, the ultimate goal is the perfect single technique.

Karate is a system that is designed to get the best out of our physical and mental form; of course it focuses on blocking, punching and kicking amongst other things, which some may label as violent and barbaric, but nevertheless, it's still the pursuit of perfection, an artistic expression full of beauty and fulfilment. It's not just that karate gives me a sense of purpose in my life, but the lessons I have learned, both physically and mentally have overflowed into all areas of my life.

The concept of *ikken hissatsu* can also have positive implications on your mental state. I've always had an overactive, as some may describe, energetic character. I would often go through life at one speed, like a tornado, but like all tornadoes, you eventually run out of energy and in my case spend the next few days exhausted. The *kenshusei* course didn't help my mental state, as it kept me in a constant state of alertness, and once the course finished I went into shock. An overactive mind can be both a strength and weakness. I always tried hard to calm my mind by painting and writing music, which requires a great deal of focus and concentration, but it was practicing karate every day that brought me a real sense of peace. I wouldn't like to imagine where I would be now if I didn't have this outlet.

When training in karate you work on a particular technique, combination or kata and for an hour or two you're at one with what you're doing. There are no other concerns or distractions and your mind is able to rest peacefully on the task at hand, which is something of a rarity in everyday life. Meditation is about achieving the ultimate state of peace and tranquillity, the aim being to convince your mind to think about 'nothingness,' for most, an extremely difficult thing to achieve. It takes many years of meditation practice to truly achieve this state of mind and the benefits are obvious, a chance to put your mind, that is often constantly at work, even when asleep, into a relaxed state of rejuvenation. Unfortunately, for most of us, especially when we are young, it seems almost impossible to switch off to this degree, so the next best thing is finding just one thing to put your mind on and here you will discover a great sense of relief in your life when you achieve this. The ability to switch off and focus on one thing for a given amount of time, or even nothing at all has a huge positive effect on our overall mental wellbeing.

In modern life, we have a whole range of entertainment devices to help us 'switch off,' like the TV, internet or game console. These can be great for fun and escapism, but they don't exactly allow our minds to relax in peace and tranquillity. For me, there can be nothing more satisfying than getting 'in the zone' when practicing karate. All your energy is focussed on one thing, for the good of the technique. Being focused, or 'in the zone', a phrase sometimes used in sports, actually gives our brain some much needed rest from trying to process and analyse all the information and emotion that our senses are constantly supplying it with and with this focus we can also achieve a greater degree of perfection and technical understanding. *'Ikken Hissatsu,'* therefore isn't just about achieving a perfect physical state but also a perfect mental state. Can you imagine a samurai in the midst of battle thinking about something else other than the battle, it would literally be life threatening to do so. The obvious thoughts that would run through your mind as you face a thousand ferocious samurai from an opposing clan, is 'I could get killed.'

Part of the samurai code was to value life and death in a very different way to the rest of us, that dying in battle is the most honourable death. This philosophy remained for quite some time and appeared again during the Second World War and the kamikaze pilots who would literally turn their aircraft into human torpedoes and sacrifice their lives for the greater good and the honour of dying in battle. So it would seem that to perform a task with absolute precision and determination and achieve *'ikken hissatsu,'* the mind must be active and engaged fully in that single task.

One thing more dangerous than an over active mind is an inactive mind; I have witnessed this amongst some of my friends and family, and it can be a frustrating thing to observe. Often this inactivity is preceded by complaining about a situation they are in and it seems no matter what constructive and practical advice they receive they are incapable of becoming active enough to alter their situation and sure enough, six months later when you meet again, very little has changed and they are still complaining about the same things. This inactivity is of course very dangerous in karate, and often students seem paralysed to take the next step forward—especially those that have trained for many years and fallen into a rut, so to speak. There are also those that don't realise that they have stopped moving forward, as if they are just treading water to keep their head from going under. Poor fitness in karate can compound this problem. It's a common misconception that karate will make you fit; it will, of course, improve your fitness to a certain level as our body and organs are initially shocked by being introduced to a new form of exercise, but eventually it will get used to training twice a week for an hour or two. Further improvements can only come as we continue to exert ourselves more than our usual routine. There are also different types of fitness; that's why we can wake up the next day after two hours of karate and feel fine, but run around a football pitch or tennis court for an hour and find that our body has a whole different level of pain.

Students that succeed in obtaining their *shodan* (1st degree black belt) can become vulnerable to an inactive mind and attitude. Naturally they have reached a very respectable peak, but sometimes wearing a black belt can breed complacency. The focus shouldn't be on what level we are, but what level we want to be and for most, that level is usually up. Therefore it requires a new game plan, a greater level of enthusiasm and commitment; I will omit to using the word 'desire' as I have met people with the greatest amount of 'desire.' Desire to become world champion, desire to run their own business, desire to travel the world, but all desire gives them is the ability to talk passionately about what they want to do, but will always put off until tomorrow.

Determination is the key to getting things done and it's unmistakable when you see that glint of determination in someone's eye.

I've seen it in the man facing me in the arena, I've seen it in my children's eyes when they are desperate to win the game, I've even seen it my wife's eyes when she wants to win an argument!

There is a big difference between desire and determination; of course, we need to desire something first before we can become determined, but it's amazing how many people live their lives desiring something but never become determined enough to do anything about it. Motivation is also one of those words linked to achievement and success, but I think it's a false prophet. We all experience motivation at certain points of the day, week, month, year and throughout life and we are very grateful for it. It drives us to stay longer in the gym, run longer in the park, study harder in the library, but it has one major shortfall. For most of us, it has no consistency. In fact, especially as our motivational levels waver they deteriorate further and further. For example, three weeks have passed since going to the dojo, so naturally our level drops off. Upon returning, everything feels more difficult due to a lack of practice, further demotivating us in training. In some cases, when students have longer absences from the dojo, sometimes through injury, work commitments or because at that point, they don't have the motivation required to attend. However, something prompts their motivation into action and they return to the dojo after a long absence and are sometimes shocked at how far their level has dropped. I've known students to return for one lesson after a year's absence to be so shocked by the deterioration of their level, they never return again to the dojo. Though equally, I've also had students that realise how much their level has dropped and this drives their determination to regain themselves. We are all very different.

If desire and motivation are not enough to keep us training regularly or enough to get us from *shodan* (1st degree) to *nidan* (2nd degree) then what can we rely on to get us there. There is only one reliable way to succeed at something and that's habit. Make it a habit. It sounds obvious, but some habits are never questioned.

I have a habit of waking up in the morning and enjoying a cup of tea. I've done it since I was a child and for me, it comes with growing up in Darjeeling, one of the most famous tea making regions of the world. I never have a discussion with myself as to whether I will have a cup of tea in the morning or not, I just go through the motions and make one. I don't give myself a choice and I don't wait until I'm adequately motivated enough to make one. Of course it's easy to stick to this habit because drinking tea is seen as a pleasurable experience and doesn't require a major amount of effort. It's a habit that will continue until I die, but it's not a pleasure for everyone. I know people that like tea and will drink it on occasion, but maybe they have a habit of fixing themselves an orange juice in the morning instead. Everyone forms different habits but we do have control over which habits we form, even addictive ones like smoking. The big question is, how do we make something a habit? How to create a habit of removing oneself from the sofa and going to a dojo to train hard for a couple of hours, even when it means running the risk of getting a fist or foot in the head for our troubles.

One of the first steps to achieving a habit is to see and feel the pleasure in what we are doing, undoubtedly an obvious point but the process to achieving this isn't always so obvious. Drinking tea can be an obvious pleasurable experience, but what about the things that aren't obviously pleasurable to us?

For me, how could I possibly see the pleasure in studying a subject like math? How could I possibly learn how to enjoy it? Well, math is no different from puzzle solving, and many people gain pleasure from working something out. The problem with math exists if you can't figure it out, that's why it's important to start small when studying something new. In the case of math, you start with a simple calculation like 15 divided by 5 and take pleasure from working it out. This is how we begin to help children to understand; with simple arithmetic first. Start with advanced algebra, and you are heading for a world of frustration and even self-loathing. You will hate math and then there is absolutely no way the study of math will ever become a habit that will help you achieve your desired goal of becoming an eminent mathematician or a fighter pilot. We would all derive great pleasure from understanding algebra in a week, but the pleasure comes from the learning process, the joy of understanding and that feeling of progress being made. We can all learn algebra but not in one giant step, only in very small incremental steps spread over time, for some of us, a long period of time. For some reason we seem to forget this concept when we become teenagers and adults. We want to know now! We want to understand now! And, if we don't understand quickly enough then we give up and move on to something easier.

Doing things out of habit will lead to consistency and repetition, which is the key to perfection. Habits are only formed from pleasurable things. We all gain pleasure from learning, understanding and that feeling of making progress. Math can be pleasurable, and if math can be pleasurable then many other things can also be pleasurable. Going to the dojo to improve your technique, working on a kick and working towards perfection in a kata can all be seen as pleasurable and therefore the habit of training at these things will be formed. Of course bad habits can also form, and most often people don't realise this until it's too late and they have developed an addiction.

An addiction implies some sense of 'not being able to function without it,' an uncontrollable desire. Most people would agree that being addicted is a negative character trait and this is understandable when you consider things like being addicted to smoking, drinking and gambling. I would say that I'm addicted to karate in the sense that I wouldn't function well without it. However, addiction can imply an obsessive and unhealthy attitude towards something, and could lead to losing control, like a lady who is so passionate about having a slim figure that eventually leads to an addiction to losing weight and the development of life-threatening illnesses like anorexia. Another equally applicable example could be the student who is obsessed with getting top grades and push themselves to the brink of a mental breakdown.

The important lesson when developing a habit is to keep a healthy balance and develop it slowly. If you begin karate by training six hours a day, then you start from a very difficult position. Trying to build a habit of six hours a day will be self-defeating. Maybe you achieve it the first day, thanks to a high level of motivation, but the next day you can only manage four hours of training. You feel deflated that the path you set for yourself has already ended in failure. Failure that you only managed four hours of training when you were supposed to do six hours. Sounds crazy to consider this as failure, but in effect, it is; you failed by two hours. The point is to not set yourself up for failure in the first place. Challenge yourself by all means, but start off by making that first challenge attainable, otherwise you end up giving up at the first hurdle. Ultimately a habit forms slowly over time, if it's allowed to. I didn't make a conscious decision to drink tea every morning for the rest of my life. I just began by following my parents as a child (lots of our habits are formed by observing others, especially our parents) so I could say it felt like a natural habit.

My karate habit initially formed out of having a schedule dictated by work commitments. It began by attending the dojo for an hour here and there, then built up gradually for a few hours a day. During *kenshusei* this changed drastically and it became more of a job than a habit, in the sense that I felt pressure externally to attend the dojo. That pressure came from the knowledge that I would be expelled from the course if I didn't attend every day. This is why work isn't directly seen as a habit that you have developed, but something that has been forced upon you. However, often when people reach retirement they find certain habits surrounded with work very difficult to break. In fact, if you apply the idea of finding little pleasures in your work and taking pride in what you are doing; then even work can become pleasurable and given the choice, a habit you would continue with even if you suddenly became independently wealthy.

To follow a schedule that is dictated to you is based on fear, like we do with work, and such as I did on the *kenshusei*. The fear is from losing something if that schedule is not fulfilled, but to follow a schedule laid down by yourself with no reprisals for breaking, apart from the feeling of guilt and failure, can be more difficult. The way to succeed is to be self-disciplined and for some people this seems very easy, but for the rest of us, it can be as difficult a task as remaining constantly motivated.

The answer once again lies in small steps. Make sure you plan a schedule that is achievable to where you are in life at the moment. If you feel you have low energy or feeling a bit depressed, then don't plan a 10k jog round the park, but instead a 30 minute brisk walk, then next week build to a 30 minute light jog. It won't be long before you're running 20k without even realising it, and soon it's a matter of habit.

Building *on* a habit is just as important as building *a* habit. For instance, you might jog regularly and have a habit of doing three 10k jogs a week, which is a very good habit for improving and then maintaining your health. Your body will adjust comfortably to this level if consistency is achieved. However, once this level is achieved your fitness will be maintained and not necessarily improved any more. If you are in your later years, then this might be a desirable habit, to maintain your health. If you plan to start running marathons then the original habit of running 10k three times a week must be built upon, increasing to 12k and so on. The initial habit of coming home from work and getting into your running gear still remains the same, but a small and manageable adjustment has been made that will soon go unnoticed. You will forget that your evening run used to last 45 minutes, but instead now lasts 1 hour. Self-discipline, like motivation is also a fragile beast. Success in this area breeds further success but likewise, failure breeds further failure.

If you notice that you are not achieving your schedule or set of goals and you've already broken it many times, then you have unwittingly formed a habit of breaking your schedule or promises made to yourself. You will feel bad, and probably forgive yourself by saying that the schedule was too tough or the goals were too high to begin with. It's not necessarily a bad thing to forgive yourself as opposed to mentally beating yourself up, but better to not set yourself up for failure in the first place. Start with a thirty-minute brisk walk, and when you're standing in the shower afterwards with a smile on your face and thinking, 'Yes! I did it,' you're more likely to feel other peaks are achievable and continue along your path of improvement. This seems to hold true in every discipline and it comes from the old adage, 'Don't run before you can walk'. I guess if we try and run before walking and stumble and fall, we can do a lot of damage both mentally and physically.

A friend of mine once told me how excited he was at the prospect of surfing for the first time. He watched with amazement and admiration all the surfers on his local beach gracefully cutting across a barrel shaped wave, some even reaching back into the wave, playfully stroking this mighty force of nature as it powers you towards the shore. I'm sure a beautiful sight and experience. He hired a board one day and set about achieving this challenging feat. Within the first ten minutes he was back on the beach rubbing his bruised head never to take to a board to the surf again. He had clearly failed to take the first steps and literally thrown himself in the deep end and learnt the true force of the wave through the pain of a fibreglass board hitting him on the head. Had he learnt the basics first, selected the right kind of board and stuck to the white water, he may well have been still surfing today, he may even have been a world-champion surfer. It seems part of modern life to want things and to have them quickly, so naturally we take a bigger step than we can handle which ultimately becomes self-defeating.

A lesson our parents try from an early age to teach us is the lesson of patience. At a young age, we are excited by the prospect of having something we want but don't always understand the necessary steps to get it. We often jump around excitedly, even throwing tantrum until we get what we want. In adulthood we of course develop more patience and understanding for having things, but this doesn't mean we always develop enough patience to achieve the more difficult things we want. In the case of dieting, it seems easy to go without a snack and just wait patiently for dinner, but to spend months, even years patiently waiting and working towards that final goal requires a lot of patience and effort, sometimes it's easy to lose track of why we started something, or we get distracted along the way. Dieting is a good example of how the mind sometimes works. To lose weight naturally usually requires two things, a reduction in your calorie intake and increased amounts of exercise. To remove something from your daily routine that you love, like ice-cream or some other high calorie treat, and then to also add something to your daily routine that you're not used to, like exercise can be a very uncomfortable life change for some people.

As much as I love karate the three years of full time training on the *kenshusei* course completely pushed me out of my comfort zone and there were moments when I really questioned if I could continue with the course. The things that often kept me going was the occasional recognition of progress being made. Usually this was my own self-recognition when I performed a kata and felt that I had made some improvements, or I fought one of my fellow students and felt I had more of the upper hand. It was rare that a sensei would give praise but when it did happen it felt like a huge reward and of course spurred me on. I believe recognition can play a big part on how far we go along the path to achieving things, after all we are only human, we have ego's and we need to be told, by ourselves (self-recognition) and often more importantly, by others (external recognition) that we are doing well and should continue you on. Can you imagine how encouraging it is to stand on the bathroom scales after three weeks of exercise and dieting and see a significant loss of weight, or even have someone compliment you on your slimmer figure. Recognition is important when you're trying really hard to achieve something and reach a goal and it also gives you confidence and holds at bay those nagging feelings of self-doubt.

Chapter 13 Recognition

Patience, discipline and habit forming are some of the ingredients to success and the pursuit of perfection, but we shouldn't underestimate the importance of 'recognition.' Recognition is important in driving us forward, both self-recognition (internal) and external recognition. Which aspect of recognition is more important depends on the type of character you are. It's possible we've all met people where it seems everything they do is to seek approval and admiration from others, so require a significant amount of external recognition to sometimes achieve their goals. There are also those that struggle to feel any self-recognition, achieving something that is seen as very admirable to others but for them they dismiss as insignificant, almost as though it doesn't rate high enough on their own self-recognition scale. For the majority of us though, we probably require a mixture of them both to push us along the path to achieving our goals.

I believe the true test of spirit is how far you push yourself when you're faced with no recognition, or put more simply, no reward for your efforts. This is probably where most people give up and fail to reach that goal. If the scales had just been a few pounds under after three weeks of exercise and dieting, or the test score had been higher after hours and hours of intense study. Understandably, it can be a very bitter pill to swallow when all your efforts amount to nothing. I felt this during periods of the *kenshusei* course, hours and hours of blood sweat and internal tears and still I couldn't land a punch on any of the sensei's, it seemed no matter how hard I trained I would still go along the line and take the same level of beating from each of the sensei's present in the dojo that day. If I had been improving then they were also improving at an equal rate as I had no recognition that my level had made any improvement and as I stood in the shower at the end of training, nursing my bruises I sometimes felt an incredible sense of hopelessness in my cause to become a professional karate instructor. How could it ever be possible when the sensei's I'm trying to emulate seem to make such easy work of me.

I also experienced this feeling with my restaurant business, especially the second time round when I opened a restaurant in a less vibrant area of Tokyo, and it seemed to take forever to achieve any measure of success, hours and hours of sitting alone in my restaurant wondering if I will ever get enough customers to be able to pay the rent and live a normal life. Sometimes things take a lot longer than expected and it's a real test of character to have the confidence to continue on when there doesn't even seem like a glimmer of hope.

Hopelessness is very difficult emotion to overcome and if you set your challenge too high then you're more likely to encounter it. I know of many friends that have gone into business for themselves, hoping to break free from the rat race and become rich. However, they often end up working longer hours and for less money, it seems the market or their industry hasn't recognised them and rewarded them with more money and free time. More hours spent studying doesn't always equate to higher grades, greater devotion and affection to a loved one doesn't always guarantee their returned love and more intense karate training doesn't always mean you will win that karate tournament, but I think it's true of most people, that we need some measure of recognition because if we can recognise that progress is being made then we have some hope that what we are working so hard to achieve is actually achievable. During the final year of the *kenshusei* course I received some recognition for my efforts and won the *kumite* international championship in Kuwait.

Winning this championship confirmed to me that all my hard work and sacrifice had been for something, and had not been in vain, but more importantly I shouldn't lose faith in what can be achieved if you're willing to work hard and commit yourself fully. However, there is an important lesson to be learnt with recognition and it relates to expectations.

When I first entered the JKA dojo and asked Tanaka-sensei if I could train I was full of excitement and enthusiasm and I told him I would like to get my *shodan* in two months. He smiled politely and said this is not possible and sure enough after two months I didn't receive my *shodan*. I then returned home to Darjeeling feeling as though I had failed and my efforts in Japan had not been recognised with the reward of a black belt. The townspeople also didn't recognise my achievement of going to train in Japan for six months, not because they were mean and incapable of complimenting achievement but because I had built not only my own expectations but also theirs, so everyone, including my family expected me to bring home a black belt. I failed to recognise what I had truly achieved during my first six months in Japan because my expectations were set far too high. Luckily for me it didn't deter me from returning and eventually reaching the goal of a black belt from the JKA.

Undertaking any discipline or challenge requires not only good physical development and mental focus, but also how we manage our overall mental state. It's our mental state that will determine how long and how hard we work at something and ultimately whether we see it through to our goal, or whether we give up. The mind must be healthy, free and not restrained by things like fear and doubt as these ultimately place further obstacles in front of us, and whilst human emotions such as praise and recognition need to be considered they can be tempered by having the right level of expectation in place.

The essence of good karate technique is similar to how we manage our life. In karate, we remain relaxed but poised. Every part of our body is relaxed, but not in any way switched off. It's free of tension and ready to react to whatever is thrown at it. The mind should be held in a similar state, relaxed, alert and ready to respond to anything. A mind, just like the body, when in a state of tension doesn't perform to its best. It's tense and slow to react, and will no doubt miss opportunities as well as suffer blows from a lack of early action. An example of this can often be found in the workplace. Often people work under a state of stress and high tension, which often means they are incapable of giving their best.

Too busy looking over their shoulder concerned about the criticism they might receive from their boss or other colleagues.

A person with a relaxed mind will react quickly to this criticism and formulate ideas and a plan to improve their situation. They will be creative, and instead of curling up in a ball of failure will work patiently to find a solution. This is essentially the essence of good karate, relaxed and poised, open to receiving all the necessary information and then ready to react accordingly. In a tournament, if you stand in a fixed stance, tense and concerned about taking a hit, then your resources are tied up in worrying about this, instead of cautiously surveying the situation and deciding on a plan of action.

I made this point to one of my students one day who came to train with me in the mountains. As well as karate we worked on our stamina and agility by climbing mountains and jumping rocks along a fast flowing river near my house. We worked further and further up the river until the jumps became wider and riskier. My student stopped, frozen on a rock unable to make a jump to a small slanted rock that jutted out the water in a section of fast flowing rapids. Up until that point he had managed to jump quite successfully with his own technique. I returned to him and we made our way back to the other side of the bank where I taught him how to jump and land successfully on this type of rock formation. He practiced the jumping technique successfully on several similar landing points, but once again froze at the same rock. I asked him what the problem was, and he explained that although the face of the rock he wanted to land on and the distance was similar to the other rocks he had been practicing on, it was obvious that if he failed to land correctly on this particular rock there would be greater consequences, he would fall into the rapids and bang his head, resulting in a serious injury.

His problem was that he allowed his mind to complicate things by thinking about all the different outcomes instead of the outcome he wanted. I learnt this when I opened my restaurant in Komagome and again in Otsuka. Instead of focusing on the outcome I wanted for my restaurants, I instead filled my mind with self-doubt and complication.

I encouraged my student to think only about the rock he was about to land successfully on, to reach out mentally to the rock, have a conversation with the rock, ultimately to rid his mind of all other conversations that were going on in his head at that point, especially the one he was having with himself about falling and injuring himself. He eventually focused his mind to only this task and jumped successfully, continuing on, to even more difficult rocks.

This example illustrates how powerful the mind can be in overcoming obstacles but also how powerful the mind is in creating obstacles. I have done it so much in my life, especially during my three years on the *kenshusei* course. Instead of just enjoying the two-week Christmas break during my first year of the *kenshusei* I allowed my mind to drift off and ponder all the anxiety that revolved around returning to training, and therefore not enjoying my time off from training. Both my mind and body failed to receive some much-needed rest and recuperation during that break.

My mind was often distracted when I was fighting with one sensei during the *kenshusei*, distracted at the possibility of getting hit (often a self-fulfilling prophecy) and which sensei I would be fighting next, not to mention also focusing on how utterly exhausted I felt. Had I mastered the control of my mind at this young age I might have escaped some of the punishment I experienced during that time and also enjoyed the Christmas break!

It was the same when I first opened a restaurant; worrying and sometimes visualising that no customers would turn up, or I wouldn't have enough ingredients to satisfy the demand if too many customers turned up. It's very easy to get wrapped up in thinking about all the possible outcomes and to not concentrate on the desired outcome, and even if things work out you fail to enjoy the experience because you were too busy concerning yourself about all manner of things.

Having a tight mind isn't an easy thing to achieve. Just step out your comfort zone and do something daring, like jump out of a plane, bungee jump or even approach that special person you like for a date and you will quickly see how your mind starts racing in all kinds of directions. I'm not claiming I've mastered the ability to control my mind to remain tight and focused, but it has most definitely improved since my *kenshusei* days and it's something I still continue to work on. In fact, to be able to focus with all your concentration on one thing isn't the highest peak in terms of mastering the mind. There is a very important concept in budo called *mushin*.

Mushin, shortened from the Zen expression, *mushin no shin*, which roughly translated means, 'the mind without mind,' refers to a mind without thoughts, able to operate with complete freedom and intuitively. If you're an experienced driver of a manual car you will understand this concept immediately.

When you first learn to drive, you make a conscious effort to listen to the sound of the engine, push the clutch down and then slide the gear stick across to the next gear. However, after many years of doing this, often on a daily basis, the whole process is carried out subconsciously, freeing your mind to act intuitively and allowing you to make a smooth transition through the gears.

If you apply this concept to karate and other martial arts, the benefits are obvious, especially in regards to combat. During my tournament days and fighting against some of the best *karateka* in the world, it would have been impossible for me to compete at this level if my mind hadn't been relaxed and free. At this level, to try and process the information of a punch descending upon you at great speed and then to think, I must block and retaliate, the fight is already lost. Similar to the principle of changing gear in a car, the only way we could achieve a response to an attack was to practice defending that attack over and over again. Repetition is not only the key to perfecting a technique, it's also the key to mental conditioning, the essence of *mushin*: To know the attack, technique or situation with such familiarity that your mind no longer seems engaged in the process of reaction. Of course the mind is always engaged, but in the area of your subconscious which has a far greater reaction speed.

Chapter 14 Zen Ku Mon

The techniques I will demonstrate in the following chapters are an attempt to show you the importance of how the body works to create that perfect technique. The words I have just written are an attempt to pass on what I understand about the mind and how it can work for us and also work against us. In this book I have also tried to document my journey into karate and then my life in karate, as well as I what I know of its history, in essence I've tried to demonstrate the true spirit of *karate-do*. When the mind, body and spirit come together much can be accomplished in life and in karate, good *kime* is achieved.

Kime, from a physical perspective is where the muscles remain relaxed until the moment of impact and upon impact the muscles are tightened, including the abdomen to exhale air from the body, which further tightens the muscles. *Kime* also refers to complete focus, both mentally and physically. For me, I also include spiritually, or should I say the spirit of shotokan karate, to incorporate concepts like *ikken hissatsu* and *mushin*. When the mind, body and spirit work together then good *kime* will manifest.

Funakoshi-sensei believed that karate could be more than just empty hand combat, he believed and proved that with honest and diligent study of shotokan karate huge benefits to not only your physical and mental being could be achieved. He also believed passionately that the study of shotokan would help develop good character. In his book, 'The Twenty Guiding Principles of Karate,' Funakoshi-sensei laid down his fundamental beliefs in karate and today in many dojo across the world the *dojo-kun* is recited at the end of each lesson to remind ourselves about the true meaning of karate.

道場訓
DOJO-KUN

一、人格完成に努るむこと
Hitotsu _ Jinkaku kansei ni tsutomuru koto
One thing _ Seek perfection of character

一、誠の道を守ること
Hitotsu _ Makotono michi o mamoru koto
One thing _ Be sincere

一、努力の精神を養うこと
Hitotsu _ Doryoku no seishin o yashinau koto
One thing _ Put maximum effort into everything you do

一、礼儀を重んずること
Hitotsu _ Reigi o omonzuru koto
One thing _ Respect others

一、血気の勇を戒むること
Hitotsu _ Kekki no yuu o imashimuru koto
One thing _ Develop self-control

I am also passionate that karate is more than just a system of combat, and have attempted in this book to show the profound and continued effect it has on my life. I don't claim my philosophy is unique, as I'm sure you can find similar ideas in many books that are available, but my beliefs come from living, experiencing and sharing with others. I've never actually read a book on philosophy, but had many conversations with people that have. Naturally my ideas have been formed from not just my experience, but also from deep discussions with others. I've always been keen to draw a conclusion, not necessarily and end, as I still seek further enlightenment, but a way of summing up where I am today. I would often think about this when walking in the mountains and it was during these walks I came up with a word to optimise how I felt about my life in karate. This word is *zen-ku-mon*.

Zen refers to meditation and the quest to focus our mind in the pursuit of mastering something in life. It's the very basics of achieving something. A strong and focused mind builds the base for achievement. From a physical and karate perspective, *zen* is the basics that builds the foundations for all possibilities.

Ku refers to the empty sky and out attempt to keep the mind clear of obstructions. To keep life simplistic and natural so you can react effortlessly and ideally from a state of *mushin*, to everything that life throws at you.

Mon refers to the gate, philosophically, the gate by which we enter this world and the gate by which we leave. Indicating that there is a start and finish to everything. Together, zen-ku-mon gives meaning and guidance to me in both life and karate.

Chapter 15 Pre Training Technique

Developing the hip

One of the most important aspects of shotokan karate is hip movement and for a technique to be truly effective the hip needs to operate in the correct manner. There are many styles of karate that believe the hips plays an important role in a technique but I feel shotokan is one of the few styles that actually teaches its student how to develop good hip mobility and therefore give the student a chance to use their hips correctly within the technique. Many karate practitioners prefer to teach the overall technique with lots of repetition and hope that the student's hip movement develops as a result of repetition. I believe this can develop bad habits when executing a karate technique and with students natural desire for speed and to move on to new and exciting techniques, this bad habit is rarely corrected and the hips are never used correctly leading to techniques that look fast but are ultimately weak.

In order to develop your karate to an effective level you have to develop movements that presuppose the technique, or pre technique exercises if you prefer. One of the most important is hip movement. Here are a number of exercises to develop correct hip movement:

Hanmi shomen hip whip

Stage 1

Standing in *zenkutsu dachi* with the hips facing forward (*shomen*) and the lower body relaxed but taut, slowly turn the hips to the side to an open position (*hanmi*.) There are a number of important points to check here:

1) Do not allow your hips to rise. Keep them in a level position as they turn so your belt remains horizontal and not sloped.

2) Make sure your front knee doesn't move. It will have a tendency to pull inwards but draw strength from your feet through the floor and keep the

knee tightly fixed forward. The inside of your thighs should also feel taut and strong which should also help prevent the knee from moving.

3) Both feet should remain fixed to the floor and shouldn't move. There will be a tendency for the rear foot to open outwards but make sure this doesn't happen.

4) It's natural for your rear knee to open outwards with the hip; this is fine but make sure it snaps back into position when your hips return to *shomen*. This is the key to drawing power from the floor through your rear leg and into your hips.

Once you are satisfied with your hips in *hanmi* position return them slowly to *shomen* position paying special attention to the point just made about the rear knee also returning to a forward position.

Common errors:

1) Front knee moving

2) Back foot moving

3) Upper body moving, especially the head (head movement clearly telegraphs to an opponent your intentions)

4) Over-turning the hip when returning to shomen

5) Raising the rear heel.

Stage 2

Now your hips have been conditioned to the correct movement, introduce more speed snapping your hips from *shomen* to *hanmi* pausing to check your hip position against the important points made earlier, before snapping the hips back to shomen.

Stage 3

Finally you are ready to practice the whole movement of snapping your hips from *shomen* to *hanmi* and back to *shomen* with one quick and effortless motion. It's a simple rule, the more you practice this exercise the more freely your hips will move and the better your techniques will become.

When you see this done correctly you will observe the hips snapping open and closed as though its independent to the rest of the body, you could almost liken the movement to a door being flung open and slammed closed while the door frame and hinge remains stable and strong.

As your hip mobility improves from this exercise you will notice a huge difference in your technique, this will be especially noticeable when executing a combination of techniques, for example *age uke* (upper block) *gyaku zuki* (reverse punch.) The power you will feel when you drive your blocking arm upwards to meet the attack as your hips snaps into *hanmi* position and then the power you feel as your hips snaps back into *shomen* position, along with your rear knee snapping forward to straighten the rear leg, as you drive the *gyaku zuki* with more power than you have previously experienced. You will begin to understand why correct hip movement is so important to shotokan karate.

Squat to forward hip snap

As well as the hips being fully engaged when moving from *shomen* to *hanmi* and then back to *shomen* it's equally important to engage the hips fully when moving forward. It may seem natural that the hips are forward so therefore generating power forward, but often the hips are being weakly applied, either due to being too relaxed and slightly rotating down, or over tensed and rotating upwards. This exercise is designed to remedy that problem.

From the squat position keep your hips relaxed but your legs taut and prepared to spring upwards. Spring forward into *zenkutsu dachi*, driving the hips forward and finishing with your rear leg straight and a sense of conveying your energy forward. Be careful not to rotate the hips down or up slightly, concentrate on projecting them forward horizontally. Repeat on both sides and you will also discover the leg strengthening benefits of this exercise. Try to keep your hips and upper body as relaxed as possible when in the squat position, but when you snap into *zenkutsu dachi* make sure your hips and abdominal muscles are taut.

Hip snap advanced

This exercise is also designed to condition your hips to snap forward in a powerful way. It's designed to stop your hips from becoming sluggish when executing a forward technique. Sometimes you can tell when the hip is not being used to its full potential by the fact that the hips slightly slope downwards in a forward position. It's equally important not to over snap the hip and have it facing upwards. It must move forward with complete forward momentum. If the hip is slightly down or up then power will be dissipated in that direction.

Kokutsu dachi snap movement

Once your hip movement improves in the *zenkutsu dachi* position you can then try it in *kokutsu dachi*. The feeling is that your hip initiates the change in direction from left facing *kokutsu dachi* to right facing *kokutsu dachi*. It would be easy to assume that the legs initiate the change in direction and it would certainly be easier to achieve this movement by using your legs and not your hips, but practicing this fast directional change using your hips will further develop your hip power.

Zenkutsu dachi slow movement training

In order to move forward correctly and with speed and power it's essential that you practice this exercise slowly as it conditions your body to understand each stage of *zenkutsu dachi*:

Stage 1 (picture 1-2)

Starting in *zenkutsu dachi*, draw the rear leg forward, bending the knee in order to keep the same height. It's important not to allow the hips to drift upwards. Your abdominal muscles must be taut, helping your body remain stable. The rest of your upper body should be relaxed and 90% of your weight should be on your supporting leg allowing the other foot to move forward whilst remaining in contact with the floor.

Stage 2 (picture 2-3)

Draw the rear foot level with the front foot. As this is just an exercise you can keep your feet apart naturally at a shoulder length width. You should begin to feel the power building in the front supporting leg like a coiled spring.

Stage 3 (picture 3-4)

The rear foot now moves forward to become the front foot with just enough weight on it to keep contact with the floor but allowing it to skate forward slowly.

Stage 4 (picture 4-5)

Finally, using the power from your rear supporting leg push into a full *zenkutsu dachi* ensuring your hips are driving forward in a powerful manner (same feeling you achieved from the squat to forward hip snap exercise.)

By doing this all slowly you can check yourself to ensure a number of things:

1) You are not moving your hips or any part of your body upwards.

2) Your hips are forward throughout the entire sequence.

3) Both knees are correctly bent to maintain a constant height throughout the sequence.

4) You maintain good posture throughout. No bending your upper body forwards or backwards.

5) You feel the build-up of power in your supporting leg before that power is used to drive forward into *zenkutsu dachi*.

I practice these exercises every class as part of the warm up and after a few months I can see significant improvements in my student's hip mobility and their understanding of how the hip should operate within each technique. These exercises have been used since the days of Nakayama sensei and quite probably before then, but it's surprising how overlooked they are in some dojo's. It seems our keenness to just get on with the technique and put it into full speed and action leads to a neglect of the finer details of body mechanics. Unfortunately for most of us, our bodies aren't naturally configured to produce good karate technique, we therefore have to teach our muscles, joints, tendons and mind the correct form before it will naturally carry out what we want to do.

In the proceeding chapters I will now show how these exercises can be used to develop some of the most important techniques in karate;

gyaku zuki (reverse punch,) *oi zuki* (forward punch,) *mae geri* (front kick,) *mawashi geri* (roundhouse kick) and combinations. These chapters do not provide a beginners guide to learning shotokan karate. New techniques are best learnt in dojos with a qualified instructor. However, Nakayama sensei's 'Best Karate' does provide the best and most comprehensive reference guide to shotokan techniques. All that I'm offering is my interpretation of the key elements of each technique and the common errors I have observed from teaching thousands of students during my karate career which is now touching forty years. My ultimate goal is to get students to think deeply about each technique and to understand the essence of shotokan karate. To encourage them to dissect a technique and understand what is necessary and also what isn't necessary, so that when they put the technique back together there is an obvious improvement in both speed and power and ultimately they are following that long and arduous path to self-perfection.

Chapter 16 Gyaku Zuki

Gyaku zuki, or reverse punch in English, is probably the most applied and successful kumite technique. If executed correctly against a *makiwara*, the sound can be likened to the clean crisp sound of a golfer striking a golf ball well, or a batsman making perfect contact with a baseball, all connecting correctly with their entire body. *Gyaku zuki* is no exception and it's at its most effective when striking the solar plexus, capable of knocking the wind out of an attacker. The science behind the punch is to bring some of the major muscles into play, for example, the *gluteus maximus*, thigh and calf muscles by twisting the hip from *hanmi* (open side position) to a *shomen* (forward position,) straightening the back leg and driving the fist forward simultaneously. This allows you to bring the power and energy from the floor, through your stance, through your hips and into the front protruding knuckles of your fist (*seiken* knuckles.) In essence you are drawing power from the floor, via large muscle groups such as the thigh and *gluteus maximus*, and focusing that power into the small area of your fist and into the target to maximise impact.

We touched on an important philosophical point in an earlier chapter that of '*Ikken Hissatsu*,' to deliver a killing blow. This was of course necessary during feudal times when the skills of the samurai were essential to their survival, knowing that it was kill or be killed whenever they drew their sword in battle. Of course, in today's civilised society there is no need for such violent determination, but '*Ikken Hissatsu*' is just as an important concept in karate-do, the way of karate, as it was to the samurai. '*Ikken Hissatsu* isn't about killing but about self-perfection, to produce the perfect technique and any practice of *gyaku zuki* should incorporate this philosophy. To search deep in your ability for the perfect technique, to find a sense of enlightenment through disciplined hard study. This is what Bodhidharma believed was essential to achieving enlightenment. Pushing the boundaries of human capabilities both physically and mentally to reach spiritual enlightenment. If we try to apply *Ikken Hissatsu* to the study of *gyaku zuki* or any other technique for that matter, we can reach a higher state of perfection and a great deal more satisfaction in what we are doing.

Gyaku zuki from zenkutsu dachi

It's useful to begin practice of *gyaku zuki* from a static stance. Keep your lower body strong and twist your hips to *hanmi* position. The front knee should remain in a fixed position, be careful not to let the knee move, especially inwards. There are many ways you can prepare the front knee from not moving. You can support the knee against a fixed object or a partner and practice rotating the hips between *hanmi* and *shomen* until your hips learn to twist independently and without moving the front knee.

If you practiced the pre technique exercises from chapter 12 you will find this technique much easier. Sometimes people worry too much about keeping the back knee locked which can destabilise the stance especially at the front knee. Let the back knee flex naturally when turning to *hanmi* in order to give complete freedom for the hips to move, this in turn will alleviate pressure on the front knee when executing *gyaku zuki*, allowing it to remain fixed and strong.

Drive the punch forward, bringing the back leg straight and the hips simultaneously into *shomen* position. Everything should now point in the direction of the target as all your power is expelled forward.

There are a number of common errors I see in students from all over the world

Over extending or leaning forward is a reoccurring problem. In attempt to reach a target that is out of distance, it's natural to want to lean in or over extend the shoulder and hips. If the target is at a greater distance than your *gyaku zuki* then you need to either adjust your distance or use a technique with a greater range, like *mae geri* (front kick). Some styles do encourage a deeper stance or an extension on the hip and shoulders to produce a longer *gyaku zuki*, there are even styles that encourage raising the rear heel in order to gain that extra distance (see picture below,) but here you trade distance with power and stability. For me, as I outlined in my life philosophy in chapter 11, simple and natural is best and I try my hardest to apply this philosophy to all my techniques.

Your goal is a simple and natural *gyaku zuki* that can be executed with speed and good timing. Technique and speed can be developed quite quickly, but good timing in the heat of kumite takes many years to develop. Having a simple and natural *gyaku zuki* will then allow you to advance on to the timing aspect of this technique more easily.

The power of the hip

Before practicing *gyaku zuki* in a *kamae* position it's important to have a feel for how the punching arm fires off the hip. The key is to be relaxed and natural. From the picture you can see that a lot of power can be generated from the hip alone. Using a partner feel the energy that you can draw from the hip and the arm without even fully extending the arm. Once you feel this, you can begin to see how drawing power up from the floor and through the back leg and firing the arm off the hip in unison will generate both speed and power with very little effort.

Gyaku zuki from kamae

Starting from a relaxed *kamae* position your weight is spread disproportionately over your rear leg, 60 – 40. The extra weight primes the rear leg in preparation for the front leg to fire forward with the hips to deliver the punch. You can see this in the second picture as the front leg begins to move forward (driven by the rear leg) and the punching arm has fired off the hip (but not twisted) to the final picture where the rear leg is now fully extended and the hips are locked forward driving the punch into the target. The point where the forearm twists, turning the knuckle over and into the target, is at the point of contact with the opponents body. This gives your forward power that extra momentum at the point of impact. There are some historical rumours that say the final twist was used to tear open the flesh in order to get at the internal organs. I'm happy to say that I've never torn open anyone's flesh by twisting at the end.

Similar to the static practice, when you land the *gyaku zuki* it's important that your front knee is strong, your hips are forward and your back leg is straight and your forearm twists at the last moment as your *seiken* knuckles drive into the solar plexus and at that moment, all the relevant muscles tighten to produce that explosive powerful punch, the essence of good *kime*.

Chapter 17 – Oi Zuki

Oi zuki is an extremely powerful technique when executed correctly. However, it is one of the hardest techniques to perform. The reason *oi zuki* is difficult is that it requires the student to travel a distance from one stance to the next. If you consider *gyaku zuki*, movement starts from the hips, which triggers the back leg and striking arm, no stance movement is required from a static *zenkutsu dachi* position. *Oi zuki* on the other hand requires the back leg to be pulled forward next to the front foot before the back leg moves on to become the front leg as power is driven from the supporting leg, hence there are a wealth of opportunities for mistakes and bad habits to develop. We will examine some of these bad habits now.

For the purpose of examining mistakes it's useful to break the sequence into four parts. Picture 1 is the static start position. In picture 2, prior to the student moving forward, a little pull back of the fist or a slight movement in the rear leg can sometimes be seen as an attempt to muster up energy for going forward, you could almost liken it to the 'wind up' motion of a punch of a poorly trained street fighter, in the sense that it goes back in order to travel forward with a greater momentum. The same could be said of this slight movement prior to executing *oi zuki*, the student pushes their energy slightly back on their rear leg to generate more power going forward. This is unnecessary and adds time to the technique and also telegraphs to an opponent that something is about to happen.

In picture 3 we see the student rise slightly as a result of the front supporting knee being too relaxed and allowing the rest of the body to rise upwards. As you can see from the red line, this motion disturbs the line of energy going forward and weakens the technique. The hips then have to move downwards, instead of just forward, to complete the technique (picture 4.)

In picture 1 you see the student has over extended by leaning forward from his waist. His back is no longer straight and his stance is unstable. The punch would be vulnerable to a counter attack where the opponent collects the punch and helps it along in order to throw the attacker off balance completely.

Picture 2 you see the opposite where the student is leaning too far back which makes it difficult for him to fully engage the hips and legs making *oi zuki* very weak. The final picture is also incorrect for *oi zuki* because the hips are left in an open *hanmi* position. There is a technique called *kizami zuki* where the hips are in a *hanmi* position, but in picture 3 the hips aren't open enough for *kizami zuki* and too open for *oi zuki*.

These are just a few of the mistakes that can be made when executing *oi zuki* which is why it's so difficult to reach a high level of perfection with this technique. When I meet a student for the first time and see them perform karate, *oi zuki* is one of the techniques that tells me a lot about their standard of karate and their understanding of shifting power from one leg to the other and how to use the hips with only forward momentum.

In order to execute any technique it's important to slow it down so you can feel each individual movement and most importantly, check to see if you're not adding any unnecessary extra movements. This type of slow movement training will help educate your muscles into getting a correct feel for the movement before doing it at full speed. It's simply a process of pulling it all apart, discarding the unwanted and then putting it back together again.

In picture 1 there is no obvious movement, but you are focusing your mind on the target and reaching that target with minimal effort and maximum speed. The key is to keep the front supporting leg at the same shape and height until picture 5, when it extends fully to become the rear leg snapping your hip in with the punch. At picture 2, 90% of your weight is on your supporting leg, but the rear foot remains in contact with the floor while it skates up next to your other leg (picture 3.) In order to achieve this without your body rising, you must ensure that your stomach muscles, your *tanden* (energy center below the abdomen) in particular, are tensed so it provides the balance and power you need to draw your leg forward.

In picture 4 there is a shift in emphasis from drawing the rear leg forward to now, pushing the front leg (previously the rear leg) forward with the pushing power of the rear leg (previously the front leg.) A lot of students miss this very important point and it explains why they lose speed and power in the final third of the technique. The supporting leg has been bent and coiled, much like a spring and now it wants to fire the whole body forward with power and speed, driving the punch into the target (picture 5.) In picture 5 you can see the correct position of the hips, still projecting forward. The rear leg is snapped straight forcing the hips to remain forward and the front leg is bent, stable and ready to support the body if another technique is required.

Chapter 18 Mae Geri

Mae geri, or front kick in English is one of the most effective and executed kicking techniques. It can be used as both a snap or thrust kick aimed at either the stomach or face. It has a lot of benefits in terms of *kumite* and street combat as it has a greater range and power than a punch and if practiced enough, can almost match the speed of a punch. As you keep a reasonable distance before executing the kick it's seen as a low risk technique as you don't commit your body into a close range area in order to execute the kick. You are of course vulnerable to counter attacks especially being spun off your line by your opponents block. There are a number of kicking techniques in Shotokan karate and *mae geri* could be seen as the least difficult, though that's not confused with the phrase 'easy to do.' It often looks easy to do and many students fail to see the details in the technique that allow for a fast and powerful kick.

I will now go through some of the common errors associated with executing *mae geri*, starting with an error that seems common to many techniques, the issue of a rising hip.

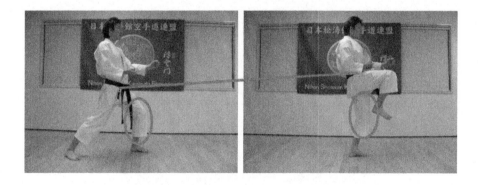

Once again the picture shows the student straightening his supporting leg, often done to get more height in the kick. As you can see from the red line, the hips rise and the energy is dissipated away from the eventual target, which is forward and not up. There are a few close contact kicks that focus on kicking upwards but *mae geri* is designed for projecting your power forward, this is why we always raise our knee to a good height before expelling the final part of the kick.

Leaning back is also a common trait as the student tries to overcompensate for poor balance or weak stomach muscles.

Leaning forward is also the result of poor balance and weak stomach muscles and above all, too much tension in the shoulders. A student practicing kicks for the first time is often not accustomed to raising their leg above their waist, so it's natural for them to try and generate enough energy to do this by tensing and using the upper body, or by leaning backwards or forwards. If advanced students make these mistakes they've either developed bad habits or they are suffering from extreme fatigue and need to improve their fitness levels.

The key to executing this technique effortlessly is to have a strong supporting leg and strong stomach muscles. When executed as a snap kick it's easy to raise the knee high enough for *chudan mae geri* and if you have a strong stance you can snap the kick out several times before returning the foot to the floor. This is a good training exercise to develop good strength and control in the core of your body. Generally with the snap *mae geri* you're focusing on the solar plexus and looking to drive the ball of the foot into the target and to retract the kick as quickly as possible so your opponent doesn't collapse over your foot. Because of the 'snap' element you place slightly more emphasis on speed than power, although that's not to say that a snapping *mae geri* to the solar plexus isn't powerful and memories of being caught perfectly by the likes of Yahara and Kagawa sensei with this kick always remind me of this point.

Thrusting *mae geri* allows for a small reduction in speed in order to increase the power in the kick. It's important when executing a thrusting *mae geri* to consider the rear supporting leg as the driving force behind the thrust. This is another reason to keep the supporting leg bent and stable. If the leg is straight or not stable any impact with a strong or large opponent will drive your supporting leg back, destabilising the whole technique and generating hardly any power.

Chapter 19 Mawashi Geri

Mawashi geri, or roundhouse kick in English is both a popular and effective kick. There are many variations of *mawashi geri* that are practiced by whole range of Martial Arts. Once again, Shotokan applies the concept of minimum movement with maximum power to bring a simple and powerful approach to *mawashi geri*. The idea is to land the kick with such speed and precision that your opponent has no time to react and the only chance you have of achieving this level of technical proficiency is to strip away all the unnecessary movements and concentrate on perfecting only the necessary. Like most techniques in Shotokan karate, it takes many years to achieve a good standard of technical proficiency in *mawashi geri*. It's important to develop good flexibility in your legs as well as good hip mobility and to start your *mawashi geri* training targeting the lower body and stomach. Once your body is familiar with the dynamics of the technique you can progress to kicking higher and from a closer range.

As with *mea geri* the supporting knee plays an important role. In the second picture you see the student lose the shape of his supporting leg which raises his whole body upwards. This is an additional unnecessary move which adds time and effort to the overall technique as well as telegraphing to your opponent that you're about to execute a technique. Remember, eyes can give you away in combat, so if your opponents eye level suddenly changes then something is about to happen. The upper body should be relaxed for most part of the technique. Only once the knee is at the side does the shoulder, along with the hip, whip the leg round to bring the flat of the foot (*haisoku*) or the ball of the foot (*chusoku*) on to the target.

Similar to *mae geri*, you keep the supporting leg strong and bent so the hips remain at a constant level where possible throughout the technique. The supporting leg, whilst taking all the weight, still allows the supporting foot to swivel naturally so the back heel finishes up almost pointing at the target. This allows the hip and upper body to move naturally without injuring the lower leg and drive the kick into the opponent. In picture 3 the kicking leg is extended to hit the target around the *chudan* (stomach) level. In order to hit the *jodan* (face) target, the hips don't rise up but instead tilt upwards towards the target, bringing the knee higher and allowing the leg to extend out higher to strike the face.

Many students are often tempted to straighten their supporting leg in order to kick higher as it brings their whole body higher and therefore closer to the target. In theory this is true but it detracts away from the efficiency and speed of a correct *mawashi geri*. With your supporting knee bent you should be able to kick your own height and if you want to go higher then more work is needed on your flexibility. I would not be looking to kick *jodan mawashi geri* to a very tall opponent, though *tobi mawashi geri* (jumping roundhouse) is possible for the more acrobatic karate student. Other styles extend their supporting leg and their kicking leg to reach some very impressive heights but the quest for height and extreme flexibility isn't the priority with shotokan karate, or at least not the shotokan I understand and believe in. As I've mentioned previously and will mention again, purely to hit home the point; shotokan is about achieving the most powerful technique with minimal movement. This is why in training it's important to dissect the whole technique to discover the true essence of that technique. Once you understand each individual move and how your body needs to work to perfect that move, you can then put everything back together and hopefully what you're left with is a clean and efficient simplified technique. Achieving this with *mawashi geri* will allow you to execute the kick with such speed and power that you will feel little difference between punching and kicking. Often kicking is seen to require more effort and timing, but if you can achieve the type of technical proficiency I outlined earlier then kicking really does become as natural and effortless as *gyaku zuki*.

Chapter 20 Continuation

When I began karate and first came to Japan to study karate at its birthplace, I often thought about what my goal was, or what peak I was trying to aspire to. These thoughts, or more accurately, obsessions, focused initially on achieving my black belt, that this was the pinnacle of karate, a reason for all the sweat and hard work that is required in such a discipline. At this early stage in my karate career I failed to see karate as a journey, a never ending journey, or as a succession of peaks to climb, progressing gently upwards. Inevitably, as your body gets older and less flexible the peaks change in shape, but are equally as challenging and important.

Gaining my *shodan* was never the pinnacle, nor winning a major world tournament or becoming chief instructor of an international karate organization. I still have peaks to master every day in the dojo. I'm still working hard on my *gyaku zuki*, *oi zuki*, *mae geri* and *mawashi geri*. Not to mention all the *kata* and *kumite* drills that requires so much dedication of time and effort to reach reasonable proficiency. However, amongst all this training it's nice to reach a level where you can afford time to work on your own signature or trade mark techniques. These aren't necessarily new and original techniques (or *kata*) but can be a combination of techniques that resonate best with your body and technical ability, a combination of techniques that help you understand the meaning of your karate training.

There are some high level karateka (and some low level for that matter) that have opted for designing their own *kata*, but for me, simplicity is best. Instead, I've worked hard to develop a combination of techniques that continue to develop my understanding of hip movement and leg power that was taught to me during those early impressionable years at the JKA dojo, shaped by the likes of Nakayama sensei and his top students, Tanaka, Asai, Abe, Osaka, Yahara, Kagawa sensei to name but a few. These combinations of technique help me understand the true essence of Shotokan karate.

The following combinations really help me develop my hip and body movement and another extremely important element, timing. As your opponent attacks with a combination of punches, each punch is met with a block followed immediately with a strike. Before I go into more detail it's important to note a key development in hip movement before I discuss the overall combination.

During chapter 13 I introduced you to many exercises that are designed to increase the full mobility of the hips, to help you gain maximum twist and therefore power. For most new students of karate they have little hip mobility or understanding of how to fully engage their hips in each technique. The exercises from chapter 13 and the proceeding techniques in the following chapters, help you rotate your hips fully to create a 'door' like effect, for example, *shomen* is the closed position, *hanmi* is the open position. The hips whip between these two positions generating maximum power. The door is either wide open or slammed closed. However, as you develop mobility in your hips and strengthen the inner core of your body, in particular the *tanden*, the power you can generate from twisting your hips greatly increases but not as a result of making such large twists, but instead smaller, faster more taut twists. It means when you observe advanced karateka you see less of a twist, or more accurately, the movement has been minimized and but with an increase in power, the essence of true Shotokan karate and the pursuit of perfection.

This allows them to move between techniques with speed, power and perfect hip alignment. This is what we aspire to achieve in karate, a slight flick of the hips generating maximum power. My signature techniques are designed to help me practice this advanced concept. However, I still practice exercise drills to open the hip fully in order to maintain that mobility.

In picture 2 my opponent attacks with *kizami tsuki* and I respond with *haito uke*, but the important focal point is that the *haito uke* is driven into my opponent's wrist area with a sharp and taut twist of my hips making the technique powerful enough to hurt the attacking arm and also to load energy for the next hip movement. In picture 3 I block *shuto gedan barai*, keeping my hips in the same position but feeling the tension developing in the core of my body. In picture 4 my hips snap open to *hanmi* position driving in *shuto yoko ganmen uchi* to the cerotic artery. In picture 5 I draw my fist back for the finishing blow and use my hips to not only drive the *uraken* into the jaw but also to shift my body out the way of further attack (picture 6.)

One of the benefits of practicing a combination of techniques is that it allows you to focus on another very important aspect of karate, tension at the end of a technique. It's a lesson you are taught early on in your karate training that the muscles should be relaxed until the final point of impact, where everything tightens as you expel the air from your body. As discussed earlier, the essence of good '*kime*.'

In reality this proves a much harder thing to achieve for many students. Often the very pensive atmosphere of the dojo, something I recall fondly from my *kenshusei* days, doesn't lend itself well to a relaxed mind or body. I see this in a lot in students and the tension they hold in their shoulders in particular, often leads to a lot of unnecessary upper body and head movement. Maintaining a relaxed mind and body until the final moment of impact is something that takes many years to master, but often it's overlooked completely, often due to other distractions in class, like a lack of fitness, attempting to learn new advanced technique or *kata*, or more sadly, just completely unaware of this important concept in karate.

These combinations of techniques allows me to take this concept further by focusing on being relaxed, tense on impact, relaxed again, tense on the next impact, relaxed again and so on. Doing this at high speed is very difficult. In fact, the only way to execute this combination at high speed is to have your body relaxed throughout the majority of the combination, so your muscles can move quickly into position before tensing at the final point of impact. This is why I practice this combination often as it covers all the important elements of Shotokan karate.

The next combination helps you develop the skill of generating power from your legs, including switching stances. The key is to keep the momentum of power going forward concentrating on snapping your rear leg and bringing your hips to *shomen* and then doing this on the other side by switching stances.

In picture 2 I attack with *chudan gyaku zuki* and then switch to *jodan gyaku zuki* as my opponent retreats (picture 3.) This switch in stance helps generate power from one *gyaku zuki* to the next whilst engaging my hips and projecting power forward into the target. The opponent retreats again and immediately I dispatch the *oi zuki* (picture 4.) The great thing about this combination is that I'm generating a lot of power from my legs and most importantly, a quick snap in my hips between each punch.

I like to call these combinations my continuation techniques as in theory if I'm using correct technique and *kime* and my partner still continues to retreat I can continue on with control, determination and *kime* until a resolution is reached, namely my attacker is disarmed. This of course is very different to the one punch principle of *'ikken hissatsu'* but still, each technique must possess good *kime* and it's only that my attacker is also very skilled that more than one technique must be employed.

If these combinations are practiced regularly you will eventually reach a state of *'mushin'* when executing the combination, so both your mind and body is completely free flowing until you reach the point where your attacker is finished. Practicing a combination of techniques like these will discourage you from stopping after your first attack, something I often witness in tournament when a competitor assumes their technique has scored.

Finally, my continuation techniques also represent the very obvious lesson with karate and life; that everything must continue on, there is always room for improvement, always a new and challenging peak to climb. A new reason to continue to enjoy life!

Postscript

Karate is one of the many paths to self-perfection, preservation and enlightenment. I love and respect karate and have therefore devoted my life to its true path. For many years I have followed this path with honesty, dedication and hard work.

I will continue to walk this never ending path to self-perfection for the rest of my life. I thank you for reading my book and hope that it has provided some light in your own journey.

Pemba Tamang (December 2014)

(For more information on Tamang Sensei and the NSKF please visit our website at www.nskf.jp)

Printed in Great Britain
by Amazon